How
Animals
Live

Edited by

Peter
Hutchinson

*a series
of volumes
describing
the behaviour
and ecology
of the animal
kingdom*

VOLUME 5

Walter M Blaney

ELSEVIER PHAIDON

Credits
to Photographers

Elsevier-Phaidon
An imprint of Phaidon Press Ltd.
Published in the United States by E.P. Dutton & Co. Inc.,
201, Park Avenue South, New York, N.Y. 10003

First published 1976
Planned and produced by
Elsevier International Projects Ltd, Oxford
© 1976 Elsevier Publishing Projects SA, Lausanne.

ISBN 0 7290 0020 6

Filmset by Keyspools Limited, Golborne, Lancashire
Printed and bound by Brepols, Turnhout - Belgium

Contents

African bush-cricket, one of several thousand species of crickets with long antennae that inhabit bushes and shrubs, the females laying their eggs in the twigs.

Introduction

There are at least five times as many different species of insects in the world today as there are of all the other animals added together. They occur almost everywhere, their populations often numbering many millions to the acre. Some species have become adapted to life in Arctic tundra, others occur in arid and scorching deserts and yet others have gained a foothold in the inhospitable wastes of Antarctica. Even in temperate climes the insects have sought out and conquered the most unlikely habitats. For example, the larvae of the Petroleum fly *Heleomyia petrolei* live in pools of crude petroleum in California, while the larvae of the related fly *Ephydra cinerea* live in the Great Salt Lake where the salinity is about six times that of sea water.

Although a few species are found in salt water, and quite a number occur in fresh water, the insects are essentially a terrestrial group. Most authorities believe that the aquatic insects of today are derived from land-dwelling ancestors. The ancestry of insects stretches back at least 400 million years; the most primitive insects known are represented by fossils from the Devonian period, and were found in flint-like rock at Rhynie in Scotland. These ancient insects showed the characteristic features which we recognise in insects today; the body was divided into three regions, the head bearing antennae, the thorax with three pairs of legs, and the segmented abdomen. Although the fossil record of insects is long,

Left: Fossil of a dragonfly wing *Liassophlebia jacksoni* from the lower Jurassic, Charmouth, southern England. The earliest known insect comes from the Middle Devonian and winged insects are first found in the Upper Carboniferous but their great variety there suggests that wings evolved much earlier.

Example of a cline, that is the gradual and progressive change of one character of a species from place to place. The black or melanic form of the noctuid moth *Amathes glareosa* increases from one per cent in south Shetland to 97 per cent in the north over a distance of only 50 km.

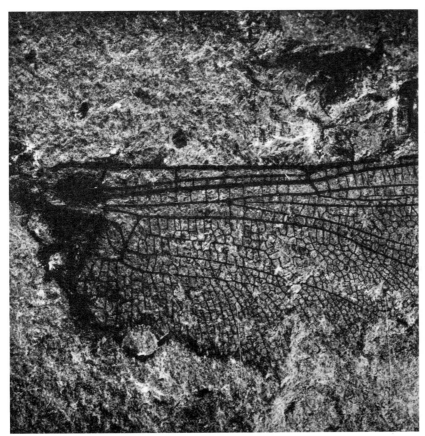

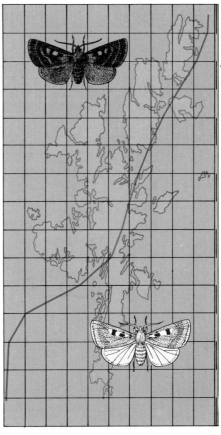

7

it is decidedly patchy because insects are often small and delicate animals and mostly live in habitats where their bodies are unlikely to be buried by sediments. Winged insects are first recorded in the Upper Carboniferous and most of the groups alive today were in existence by the end of the Permian, the age of the dinosaurs.

The diverse forms and life-styles which we see in insects today are believed to have been derived, by the process of evolution, from these ancestral forms. In the course of time the environment gradually changes and some features of an animal are more beneficial for its survival than others. Individuals with beneficial features survive and reproduce more

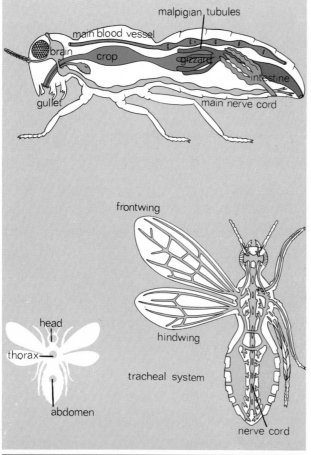

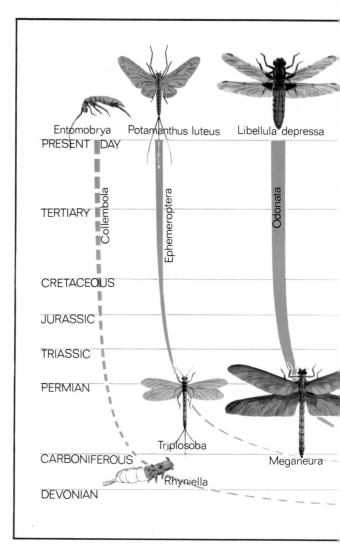

Above: Table illustrating the probable evolution of present-day insects from groups long extinct. For simplicity only a few of the present-day orders are included. The table also indicates the relationships between present and extinct groups. Insects probably evolved from a small centipede-like form without wings. Certainly the first fossil insects, from the Devonian, are wingless.

Top left: General features of the blood (red), digestive (green), nervous (orange) and tracheal (blue) systems in an insect. A typical form of the ovaries of a female is represented in purple in the upper diagram. The main blood vessel has a series of hearts which promote a sluggish circulation of blood in the general body cavity.

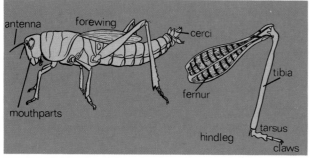

External features of an insect such as a locust. The segmental nature of the abdomen is clearly visible but the three segments of the thorax are less distinct whilst the segments of the head are so fused as to be indistinguishable externally. Right: the hind leg, showing the powerful muscles in the femur used in jumping.

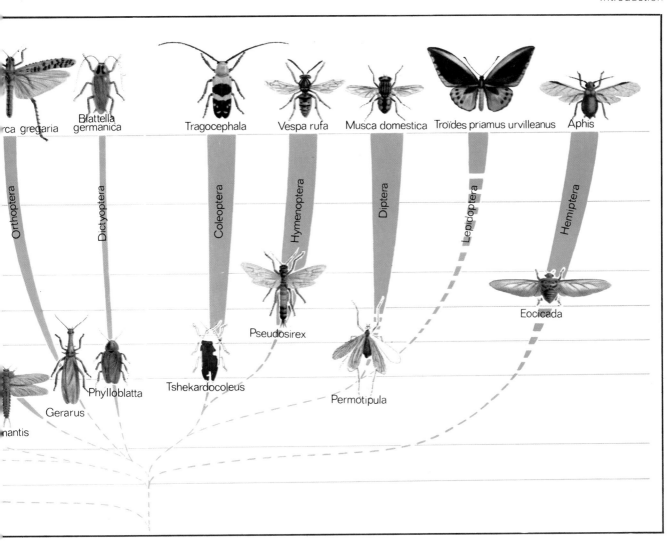

rca gregaria   Blattella germanica   Tragocephala   Vespa rufa   Musca domestica   Troïdes priamus urvilleanus   Aphis

Orthoptera   Dictyoptera   Coleoptera   Hymenoptera   Diptera   Lepidoptera   Hemiptera

Eocicada

Pseudosirex

Phylloblatta   Tshekardocoleus

Gerarus   Permotipula

nantis

successfully, and their offspring inherit the favoured characteristics. In this way a species gradually changes in step with its environment or, by the chance acquisition of a new feature, is able to exploit a new environmental niche. Conversely, since the acquisition of new features is a random process, a species may fail to change fast enough to keep up with the changing environment and as a result becomes extinct.

This sort of evolution, occurring over millions of years, can lead to changes in the insect population of the earth but does not itself result in the production of new species from existing ones. If a population is so widespread that interbreeding between individuals at opposite ends of its range becomes reduced, the characteristics of the two ends of the range may drift apart and different varieties of the species develop. If some barrier is introduced bet-

ween the two varieties, they can change to such an extent that they can no longer interbreed and new species are formed. Such a barrier may be a developing mountain range or a sea but lesser obstacles can still be effective, for example some colonies of blue butterflies of the family Lycaenidae may be divided by a hundred yards or so of long grass or other unsuitable terrain.

The Insect Plan. Thus we have today an amazing diversity of form and function in the insects, but all are variants of a basic plan. In order to appreciate the lives of insects described in subsequent chapters it would be helpful to have a picture of that basic plan. Let us look briefly then at the features of an imaginary 'typical insect'.

Compared with ourselves, insects are peculiarly constructed animals. Their skeleton, for the attachment of muscles and support of organs, is on the

Above: Pupating caterpillars and new pupae of the Small tortoiseshell butterfly hanging from their silken web. The body tissues of the fully grown larva are reorganised during the pupal stage before emergence of the adult. In the alternative type of life cycle, the young are miniature versions of the adult throughout.
Below: Of the many diverse variations on the basic insect plan, that of the stick insect is one of the most bizarre. It escapes detection by resembling an inedible object.

outside. The external covering or cuticle is, for the most part, hard and impermeable. The body is composed of a series of segments jointed together. The segmented nature of the head is not apparent for here the segments are condensed and fused together. The three segments of the thorax are indicated by the three pairs of jointed legs. The wings, where present, are not derived from limbs, as they are in birds, but are entirely different structures. Except in some very primitive insects, there are no limbs or other appendages on the abdomen apart from the reproductive organs at the end, and sometimes two small sensory structures called cerci.

The principal sensory organs, eyes, antennae and mouthparts, are borne on the head. Information from these organs is relayed to the brain, also in the head. The main nerve cord passes down the middle of the body on the underside and peripheral nerves pass into it from other sensory areas of the body, while other nerves pass outwards to control the activity of muscles. The fuel to power these muscles is derived from food digested and absorbed in the gut, a fairly simple tube running from the head to the tip of the abdomen. Oxygen used in the respiration of that food is derived from air taken in through a series of openings in the body wall. These openings are interconnected by the tubular tracheal system

The Monarch butterfly represents another variation on the basic insect plan. Scales and hairs covering the body and wings, and giving the insects its striking appearance, also serve to insulate the body and smooth the airflow over the wings. It derives protection from being distasteful to predators.

which carries air to all parts of the body. The blood system carries food materials to the various organs and waste products away. The waste products are removed by the excretory system which consists of the fine Malpighian tubules lying in a blood space and discharging into the gut.

Most insects reproduce sexually, the eggs hatching into larvae which grow by periodically shedding the outer cuticle, eventually reaching the adult state and achieving sexual maturity. Many insects have a life cycle like that of a butterfly; the eggs hatch into a worm-like larva which, when fully grown, under-

goes a drastic change during a resting or pupal stage, before becoming an adult. Alternatively, as in grasshoppers, the young are very similar in appearance to the adult and the final change is less dramatic, involving only the acquisition of functional wings and, as before, the attainment of reproductive capability.

That completes our thumb-nail sketch of the class Insecta. Now we can consider its subdivision into groups, or Orders, to see how they differ from each other and from the basic plan, and discover in more detail how insects live.

11

Classification of the Class Insecta

SUBCLASS	DIVISION	ORDER	EXAMPLES
APTERYGOTA		1 Collembola	springtails
		2 Diplura	*
		3 Thysanura	bristletails, firebrats, silverfish
		4 Protura	*
PTERYGOTA	PALEOPTERA	5 Ephemeroptera	mayflies
		6 Odonata	dragonflies, damselflies
	POLYNEOPTERA	7 Plecoptera	stoneflies
		8 Grylloblattodea	mole crickets
		9 Orthoptera	crickets, grasshoppers, locusts, bush crickets
		10 Phasmida	stick insects, leaf insects
		11 Dermaptera	earwigs
		12 Embioptera	*
		13 Dictyoptera	cockroaches, mantids
		14 Isoptera	termites
	PARANEOPTERA	15 Psocoptera	booklice
		16 Mallophaga	biting lice
		17 Anoplura (Siphunculata)	sucking lice
		18 Heteroptera	true bugs: assassin bugs, bed bugs
		19 Homoptera	plant bugs: aphids, cicadas
		20 Thysanoptera	thrips
	OLIGONEOPTERA	21 Neuroptera	lacewings, alder flies, ant lions
		22 Mecoptera	scorpion flies
		23 Lepidoptera	butterflies, moths
		24 Trichoptera	caddis flies
		25 Diptera	true flies: mosquitoes, houseflies
		26 Siphonaptera	fleas
		27 Hymenoptera	ants, bees, wasps, gall insects
		28 Coleoptera	beetles, woodworms, weevils
		29 Strepsiptera	*

* No common names

Variations on a Theme

The 'typical insect' of the last chapter is unreal but forms the basic theme on which the real insects described in this chapter are variations. This is, then, a sort of Who's Who of the insect world. To name and describe all the important insects in the world would take many volumes, so we are restricted here to saying a little about each of the orders of insects. This information is given now for those who like to know the characters before the book is read, but will perhaps be most usefully referred to from time to time as the story unfolds. The table below will give a quick guide to the different types of insects; the orders are numbered, simply for ease of reference.

The first four orders have various primitive features and, in particular, are wingless and have clearly come from wingless ancestors. They belong to the subclass APTERYGOTA (Greek *pteron* – wing, thus *apterous* – wingless). The remaining orders are the winged insects, of the subclass PTERYGOTA, although in fact some have become secondarily wingless as an adaptation to some special environment.

The PTERYGOTA can be subdivided into two groups on the basis of their larval development and, more particularly, the extent of bodily change during the process called metamorphosis during which the larva changes to an adult. Orders 5–20 form the first of these divisions and are called the Hemimetabola.

The young, often called nymphs, are similar to the adults and the nymph/adult metamorphosis is comparatively slight. This group may also be called the Exopterygota because, in the young stages, the developing wings are visible on the outside. Orders 21–29 form the second division or Holometabola in which the young differ greatly from the adults in habits and structure. The alternative name, Endopterygota, refers to the fact that the wings develop internally in the larval stages and are not visible.

A more modern subdivision, used here, is based on wing structure which is believed to be a good indicator of interrelationships. The Pterygota are divided into two major groups, the PALEOPTERA ('old wing'), which cannot fold their wings, and the NEOPTERA ('new wing') which can do so. Many orders of Paleoptera are known only as fossils. The Neoptera seem to have developed along three main lines and are grouped into the three divisions POLYNEOPTERA, PARANEOPTERA and OLIGONEOPTERA, their names being derived from features of the wing venation. Each of the insect orders will now be briefly described.

1 Collembola (springtails). It is likely that the springtails are the most numerous of all insect groups; about 2,000 species are known and there are undoubtedly many more to be discovered. They are quite small insects, most species being between

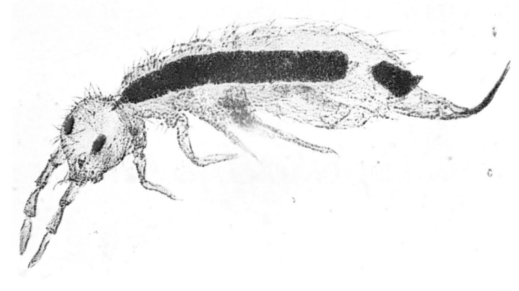

The body of a springtail, prepared for examination under a microscope, shows its very simple structure. The antennae, eyes, gut and some of the six legs are visible, as is part of the jumping organ at the tip of the abdomen.

0.04–0.1 in (1–3 mm) long. Many are white or colourless but others have various colour patterns. The head bears a pair of four-segmented antennae, and usually a number of simple eyes and mouthparts which are hidden in a pouch. The abdomen of the Collembola is unique in several respects. It has only six segments whereas that of most other insects has eleven. The pair of rudimentary legs which develops on each abdominal segment of the embryo in most insects is lost before hatching, but not so in the Collembola. Here some of these limbs, particularly at the tail end, are retained in a modified form as a jumping organ: hence the common name 'springtails'.

Collembola can only exist in humid conditions and they occur in large numbers in the soil or at the

peculiar in having the mouthparts enclosed in a deep pouch whereas in typical insects they are exposed. Individuals are rarely more than 0.2 in (5 mm) long and are found at densities of up to 5,000 per sq yd (6,000 per sq m) in some woodland soils.

3 Thysanura (bristletails, firebrats, silverfish). The Thysanura are believed to be closest to the ancestral type from which all present-day insects have evolved. There are about 400 known species. The group is widespread but seldom seen as most individuals are less than 0.4 in (10 mm) long. The most familiar example is the Silverfish *Lepisma saccharina* which is common in buildings all over the world, especially in damp places like kitchens and bathrooms. It feeds on damp and decaying organic matter and is quite harmless. The Firebrat *Thermobia domestica*, less

The bristletail *Petrobius*, showing the three antenna-like appendages at the tip of the abdomen which account for the common name of the group. *Petrobius* lives around the high tide mark and eats marine detritus and green algae which it scrapes from the rocks.

soil surface. Some live on the surface of water where their aggregations may form large grey patches. Others are littoral or marine; *Anurida maritima* is one of the few marine insects and is submerged at each high tide. Most Collembola feed on dead plant and animal material but some attack living plants. Few species are of economic importance, but the little green Lucerne flea, *Sminthurus viridis*, can be a serious pest of clover and lucerne in Australia. Some cause damage in commercial mushroom cultures and vast aggregations of several species have been known to cause blockages in sewage beds.

2 Diplura. This widespread group also lives in soil, among decaying leaves and under logs and stones. About 400 species of these slender, whitish, eyeless insects are known. The head carries long mobile antennae and often a similar pair of organs, the cerci, are borne on the end of the abdomen. In some species, the cerci are in the form of hard pincers like those of earwigs and are used to catch prey. Sometimes a poison gland, situated in the abdomen, opens at the tip of these cerci. The Diplura are

common now than years ago, lives in kitchens and bakehouses where it finds the warmth it needs for the development of its young. *Petrobius* lives around the high water mark on rocky shores but is not truly marine.

Typically the Thysanura are smooth, tapering insects covered with glistening scales. They have long, jointed antennae and leg-like appendages of unknown function on the abdomen. The three long antennae-like appendages at the tip of the abdomen account for the common name 'bristletails'. They are exceptional in continuing to moult periodically after having become adult.

4 Protura. This small group of about 200 species of wingless insects, all under 0.1 in (3 mm) long, live in the soil in all parts of the world. They were only discovered in 1907 and are in many ways different from all other groups of insects. They have no eyes and no antennae but the front pair of legs are carried above and beside the head and appear to function as antennae. Very little is known of the biology of the Protura but they can only survive in very humid

The adult of the mayfly *Ephemera danica*, one of the largest British mayflies, whose larvae live on the mud bottoms of lakes and slowly moving streams. Note the prominent 'tails' which are fringed with small bristles.

conditions and occur most commonly in the soil of deciduous woodlands.

5 Ephemeroptera (mayflies). The aquatic larvae of mayflies live in fresh water and the adults are found by river banks and lake shores. The mouthparts of adult mayflies are vestigial so they cannot feed and only live long enough to mate and lay eggs; sometimes the adult life is less than a day. It is from this ephemeral existence that the order gets its name. By contrast, the larval life can last up to three years. At the end of its aquatic life, the larva rises to the surface, the cuticle along its back splits open and the winged insect emerges. This insect has the form of an adult but is dully coloured, its wings are opaque and it cannot fly well. Within an hour or so the dun, as it is known to anglers, moults again and appears in its final form as an active, fully coloured adult with glittering translucent wings. The occurrence of an 'intermediate adult' stage is unique among insects. The wings are always held erect above the back and the fore wings are much larger than the hind wings. There are about 1,300 living species but the fossil record suggests that formerly they were much more abundant, especially in the Permian period. The aquatic larvae, or nymphs, form an important food source for larger carnivorous insects and for fishes. Fishes also take the adults of many species as they fly just above the water or submerge to lay their eggs, and the 'flies' of anglers are often modelled on species of mayfly.

6 Odonata (dragonflies, damselflies). Some 5,000 species of Odonata are known today and their unusually long and rich fossil history shows that they have remained remarkably uniform in structure since the Upper Carboniferous era, about 280 million years ago. The fauna of that time included the largest known insect, *Meganeura monyi*, which had a wing-span of 28 in (70 cm) compared with the 7·5 in (19 cm) of the largest dragonfly of today, *Megaloprepus*. The Odonata of today fall into two groups; they either hold their wings extended laterally when at rest, as in the heavily built dragonflies, or fold them above the back, as in the more slender damselflies.

Odonata are carnivorous, both as adults and larvae. The larvae, or nymphs, are fully aquatic and depend largely on vision in capturing their prey. The labium, or lower lip, has become much enlarged and modified as a grasping organ. Adult dragonflies also rely on vision, having enormous compound eyes but antennae reduced to mere spikes. The abdomen is long and narrow and the thorax is skewed forward underneath to carry the spiny legs forward to aid in grasping other insects taken on the wing.

The mating of dragonflies is unique. The male transfers sperm from his genital organs at the tip of the abdomen into a pouch under the front of the abdomen. Then, with clasping organs at the tip of his abdomen, he grasps a female by the neck and they fly off 'in tandem'. During this flight, the female curls her abdomen forward to insert the tip into his pouch and receive the sperm.

7 Plecoptera (stoneflies). Like the Odonata, the stoneflies have changed little since the Carboniferous era. They are characteristically flattened in shape with a square head bearing long antennae, two pairs of similar, transparent wings and two long prominent cerci at the tip of the abdomen. The

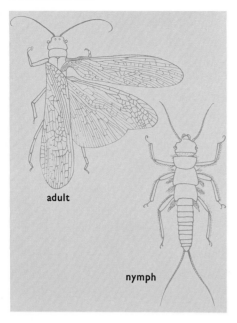

The adult and nymph of a stonefly *Perla* differ little except for the wings in the adult and the tufts of gills on the thorax of the nymph used in breathing under water. The nymphal stage can last three years.

aquatic larvae are similar to the adults but lack wings and have gills on the thorax for breathing under water. They do not readily swim and are often found beneath stones in rapidly flowing streams. Some 1,500 species have been described.

8 Grylloblattodea (mole crickets). This small order of six wingless species occur in cold mountain regions of North America, Russia and Japan. They combine features of both cockroaches and crickets and may be the surviving remnants of an ancestral stock from which these two groups have evolved.

9 Orthoptera (crickets, grasshoppers, locusts, bush crickets). There are more than 10,000 living species of orthopterans and their fossil record extends back to the Carboniferous. Typically these medium to large sized insects have the hind legs strongly developed and modified for jumping. The fore wings are leathery and protect the hind wings which are larger and folded fan-like beneath them at rest. Sometimes one or both pairs of wings may be reduced or missing. The Orthoptera have various means of producing sounds which are involved in courtship behaviour.

The order falls into two main groups, the crickets and bush crickets (tettigonids) whose antennae are long and whip-like, and the grasshoppers and locusts (acridids) whose antennae are short. The tettigonids produce their sound signals by means of a special rasp on the leathery forewings. The females usually have a conspicuous sword-like ovipositor with which they insert their eggs into soil or into the stems or leaves of plants. Crickets are usually nocturnal, living in burrows by day and eating a wide variety of plant and animal material. The House cricket *Acheta domesticus*, is sometimes sufficiently numerous indoors to be a pest. Bush crickets are similar in their habits but live in trees and bushes and are often leaf-like in appearance. The acridids produce their sounds by rubbing the hind legs against the leathery fore wings. Grasshoppers are widespread throughout the world but in

The New Zealand Smooth stick insect, *Clitarchus hookeri*. Stick insects resemble twigs in appearance and in their behaviour, remaining motionless or swaying slightly when disturbed. If excessively disturbed, they fall to the ground with legs held close to the body.

Earwigs showing sexual dimorphism. The pincers at the tip of the abdomen are nearly straight in the female (left) but are strongly curved in the male (right). The pincers are used in defensive threat and occasionally in the intricate folding of the hindwings under the tiny protective forewings.

tropical countries some species have a tendency to build up enormous, destructive swarms and are called locusts. Locusts may exist in a solitary phase for many generations, when they look and live like grasshoppers, then when conditions allow, they change to a gregarious phase, becoming brightly coloured and aggregating in swarms of many millions which, when adult, can migrate over considerable distances causing enormous damage to vegetation on the way.

10 Phasmida (stick insects, leaf insects). The phasmids are masters of disguise. The 2,000 or so species of this mainly oriental group specialize in resembling the vegetation on which they rest during the day. Even the eggs are often indistinguishable from the seeds of the host plants. The stick insects are up to 10 in (25 cm) long and are twig-like, often the thorns, buds and scale scars of real twigs being copied in remarkable detail. Many are wingless, but in others the leathery fore wings protect fanlike hind wings which may be highly coloured. The bodies of leaf insects are broad and flat and the limbs and fore wings have flat outgrowths which contribute to the leaf-like shape of the insect. The deception is completed by the remarkable detail with which leaf veins and blemishes are represented on the green surface of the insect.

11 Dermaptera (earwigs). Almost all the 900 or so species of earwig look like the familiar European species *Forficula auricularia* which is very common in gardens. They are 0·5–0·75 in (12–19 mm) long and the slender, parallel-sided abdomen bears a pair of pincers terminally. These are used in defensive

threat but are not very effective weapons. Earwigs spend a lot of time curled up in crevices, especially in flowers, and may emerge from time to time and eat holes in the petals, to the disapproval of gardeners. Though seldom seen in flight, earwigs have beautiful, semicircular hind wings. These are closed like a fan then folded over twice to fit under the short protective fore wings. The female lays her eggs in the soil and exercises parental care over them and the young larvae, collecting them together if they become dispersed. There are two groups in the tropics which have become parasitic; one on bats in Indonesia, the other on cane rats in Africa.

12 Embioptera. This small group of insects is seldom encountered. They live in groups of about 20 in silken tunnels usually built on the bark of trees, chiefly in tropical countries. The males have two pairs of membranous wings but the females are wingless. Eggs are laid in the silken tunnels and the females show parental care similar to that of earwigs. Most species are less than 0·5 in (12 mm) long and are characterized by the swollen tips of the front legs which contain the silk-producing glands.

13 Dictyoptera (cockroaches, mantids). Although quite closely related, the two sub-groups of this order, the cockroaches and the mantids, are superficially rather dissimilar. The mantids are identified by their powerful, spiny fore legs which they hold as though praying though they are in fact waiting for an insect prey to come within range. Members of this mainly tropical group rely on their well developed eyes in order to catch their prey by grasping it at lightning speed with their fore legs.

17

Giant cockroaches from tropical America, large relatives of the ordinary American cockroach. Their speed of movement, slippery bodies, unpleasant smell and the fact that they spoil food, make cockroaches rather unpopular insects. Many species will eat almost anything, including each other, as the specimen on the right here shows.

The cockroaches, which were abundant 300 million years ago, are a cosmopolitan group. They are best known by the activities of a few species which have become domesticated and distributed around the world by trade. The best known domestic pests are *Periplaneta americana*, *Blatta orientalis* and *Blattella germanica*. Unlike mantids, these cockroaches rely largely on their antennae which are long and slender and ceaselessly explore the environment. Both mantids and cockroaches lay their eggs in groups enclosed in a cuticular pouch called an oothecum. There are about 3,500 species of cockroaches and 1,800 species of mantids.

14 Isoptera (termites). About 1,700 species of termites are known and occur in the tropics and warm temperate countries. Mature adults have two similar pairs of wings which they break off after a

The dark coloured, winged adults of the termite *Neotermes* together with some whitish nymphs and eggs. After a short mating flight the adults shed their wings and resume a largely subterranean life. Termites or 'white ants' are social insects which are not at all related to ants.

Most species of booklice are winged but some are wingless or short winged. Booklice are among the few insects which spin silk when adult. This group is thought to have been, 270 million years ago, the ancestors of the present-day biting lice, sucking lice and bugs.

brief mating flight. The paired male and female seek out a nesting site in soil or wood and proceed to build up a typically fairly large colony. The mature female becomes grossly distended and is virtually an egg-laying machine. Her offspring are organized into workers and soldiers who maintain the colony for many years. With their attacks on virtually all man's fabrics and structures, the termites are among the most destructive of all insects.

15 Psocoptera (booklice). This group of over 1,000 species are pre-eminently insects of forest and woodland, living on dead or living leaves or bark. Most species are winged but many are wingless and live under bark, in birds' nests, or in houses, where the most familiar is *Liposcelis divinatorius* which lives on the mould growing on damp books.

16 Mallophaga (biting lice). The Mallophaga, of which about 2,600 species are known, are surface parasites especially of birds, but some occur on mammals. They are generally less than 0·1 in (3 mm) long and have chewing mouth-parts with which they nibble feathers and skin, rarely drawing blood. They are flattened and wingless with poorly developed eyes and soon die when separated from their hosts.

17 Anoplura or Siphunculata (sucking lice). Only some 230 species of Anoplura are known and all are blood-sucking parasites on mammals. They are similar in appearance to biting lice but their mouth-parts are minute needle-like stylets which pierce the skin. Their claws are adapted to grip firmly the hairs of their mammalian hosts. Two species are parasites on man; *Pediculus humanus* lives in the hair of the

Lice: (1–4) Sucking lice (Siphunculata). (5–6) Biting lice (Mallophaga). (1) Human head louse, 2 mm long; (2) Human body louse, 3 mm long; (3) Crab louse *Phthirus pubis* 1–1.5 mm long; (4) Dog louse *Linognathus setosus* 2 mm long; (5) Sheep louse *Trichodectes canis* 1.5 mm long; (6) Feather louse *Menopan gallinae*, 2 mm long.

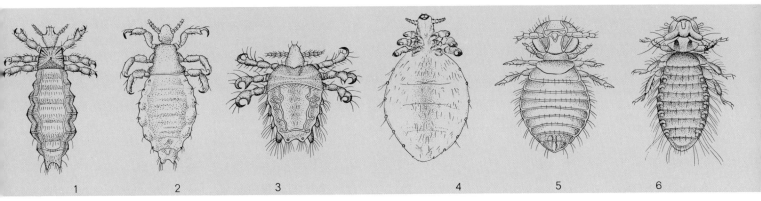

1   2   3   4   5   6

head and body, while *Phthimus pubis* usually infests the hair of the pubic regions. *Pediculus* is the carrier of some of the worst epidemic fevers of man, including epidemic typhus.

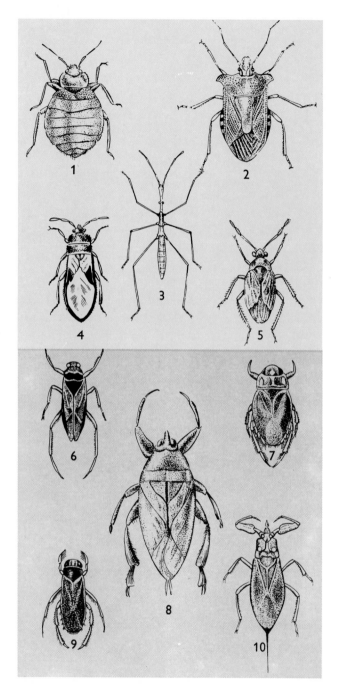

Land bugs: (1) Bed bug, (2) Shield bug *Tropicoris rufipes*, (3) Pond skater *Hydrometra stagnorum*, (4) Chinch bug *Blissus leucopterus*, (5) *Salda littoralis*, of the margins of lakes and rivers. Water bugs: (6) Backswimmer *Notonecta glauca*, (7) Saucer bug *Naucoris cimicoides*, (8) Indian water bug *Belostoma indicum*, (9) Waterboatman *Corixa geoffroyi* and (10) Water scorpion *Nepa cinerea*.

18 Heteroptera (true bugs: assassin bugs, bed bugs). There is much disagreement on how the bugs should be classified; some entomologists include them all in a single order, the Hemiptera, others recognize two orders, the Heteroptera and the Homoptera. The two orders together include some 40,000 species, all of which have mouthparts adapted for piercing and sucking. The mouthparts consist of a series of sharp, slender stylets which fit together in a tube. Most bugs feed by tapping plant juices and may inflict great damage to commercial crops, but some suck the blood of insects and higher animals, including man. They sometimes transmit diseases to the organisms on which they feed. In the Heteroptera, which includes a number of aquatic bugs, like *Notonecta*, the basal part of the fore wing is hardened and the tip of the wing is membranous.

19 Homoptera (plant bugs: aphids, cicadas). In this order the whole of the fore wing is either membranous or leathery throughout. Included here are the cicadas, noted for their shrill song, the cuckoo-spit insects, the aphids and scale insects.

20 Thysanoptera (thrips). Thrips are usually only seen on hot thundery days in summer when they migrate in large numbers. These little 'thunder blights' – few are longer than 0·02 in (0·5 mm) – alight on the hands and face and produce a very annoying tickling sensation. Only with a microscope can you make out the details of their narrow bodies and strap-like wings fringed by long hairs. At other times they live in vegetation, especially in flower heads, and a few of the 4,000 or so known species are harmful to plants.

21 Neuroptera (lacewings, alder flies, ant lions). Nearly 5,000 species of these elegant insects are known. The adults have delicate gauze-like wings and rather feeble powers of flight but the larvae are vigorous carnivores. Common examples are the green lacewing *Chrysopa*, common in gardens, and the alder fly *Sialis* which frequents the banks of sluggish streams. The larvae of the tropical and subtropical ant lions dig pits in which to trap their prey.

22 Mecoptera (scorpion flies). The most familiar example of this order of some 350 species is the scorpion fly *Panorpa*. The speckled wings, the yellow and black body and the beak-like extension of the head are unmistakable in this 0·75 in (19 mm) long insect. So too is the upturned tip of the abdomen in the male which looks alarmingly like the sting of a scorpion.

23 Lepidoptera (butterflies, moths). Butterflies, by virtue of their diurnal habits and bright colours, are

The Giant lacewing *Osinylus fulvicephalus*, which has a 2 in (5 cm) wingspan. Our best known lacewing is the green *Chrysopa flara* which comes indoors to hibernate in September and October, often in large numbers. They emerge from hibernation in the late spring.

The male Purple emperor butterfly *Apatura iris*. The beautiful colourings, typical of most butterflies, are produced by very small scales which cover the wings like tiles on a roof. Most adult butterflies live on nectar and other fruit juices.

The adult of the Caddis fly *Stenophylax permistus*. Typically drably coloured and moth-like, these insects have wings clothed with hairs. They are always found near water in which the eggs are laid and the larvae live, often concealed in a protective tube.

the best known of all insects. However, moths make up the majority of the 200,000 known species in this order, but since they are usually cryptically coloured and nocturnal they are less well known. Moths range in size from the tiny *Nepticula* with a wing-span of 0·12 in (3 mm), to the giant Atlas moth *Attacus atlas*, which measures 10 in (25 cm) across. Many moth larvae are harmful to crop plants and stored products. All Lepidoptera are characterized by the possession of scales on the wings and of mouth-parts in the form of a sucking proboscis.

24 Trichoptera (caddis flies). The wings of these moth-like insects are clothed with hairs and not scales and the mouthparts are poorly developed. The larvae of all 3,000 species are aquatic and many construct protective cases by gluing together fragments of plants and other aquatic debris.

25 Diptera (true flies: mosquitoes, houseflies). Like the Lepidoptera, the Diptera are one of the most recently evolved groups of insects. Both of

these orders have evolved along with the flowering plants and feed chiefly on nectar. The best known flies are the houseflies, blowflies, mosquitoes and midges, which attract our attention by their unwelcome activities, but in all some 85,000 species of flies are known. The larvae of Diptera play an extremely important role in the economy of nature by feeding on decaying plant and animal matter and hastening its conversion to the humus of fertile soil. The true flies are characterized by the possession of only two pairs of wings; the hind wings are reduced to knob-like organs called halteres which are involved in the control of flight.

26 Siphonaptera (fleas). This peculiar group of some 1,100 species may be related to the Diptera; the larvae of the two groups have much in common. The narrow, laterally compressed wingless bodies of fleas suit them to their parasitic life among the fur and feathers of their hosts. The mouthparts are adapted for piercing the skin and the hind legs power

Some common bumblebees of the genus *Bombyx* which have well organized colonies and division of labour. The cuckoo bees are social parasites, invading the nests of the bumblebees and utilizing their social organization. (1) Buff-tailed bumblebee *Bombus terrestris*, female left, worker centre, male right; (2) Large red-tailed bumblebee *Bombus lapidarius*, female left, male right; (3) Hill cuckoo bee *Psithyrus rupestris*; (4) Carder bee *Bombus agrorum*, queen left, worker right and (5) Cuckoo bee *Coelioxys elongata*. All natural size.

the flea in its prodigious jumps. The larvae live on debris in the nest of the host.

27 Hymenoptera (ants, bees, wasps, gall insects). This order of over 100,000 species are among the most highly evolved of insects and are, in that sense, similar to the Diptera. The hind and fore wings on each side are held together by a row of hooks and function as one. The mouthparts are mainly of the

Flies occur everywhere from tropics to arctic tundra, from mountain tops to caves and mines. The larvae of many are vitally important in re-cycling materials in nature but often the adults make life unbearable for man, by the annoyance of their bites and the diseases they transmit.

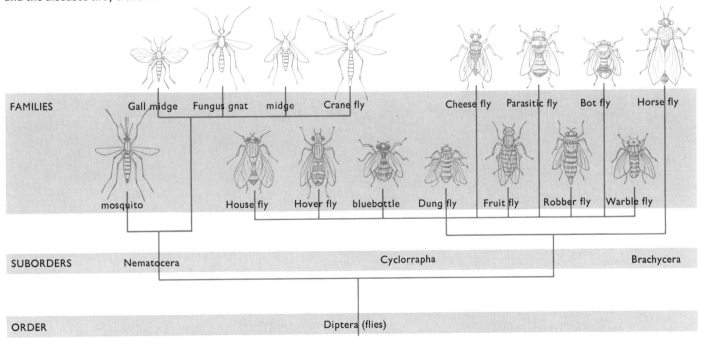

How Insects Live

biting variety but in bees are modified as a long 'tongue' to obtain nectar from flowers. The Hymenoptera fall into three main groups: the Symphyta (sawflies), Parasitica (parasitic families) and Aculeata (sting-bearing families). The sawflies are so called because the female has a saw-like ovipositor used to insert her eggs into the tissues of plants. Many of the Parasitica lay their eggs in the larvae of other insects. The Symphyta and Parasitica include species whose larvae provoke plants into producing characteristic swellings called galls. The Acuelata are the ants, bees and wasps, some of which have evolved a highly organized social life with caste systems in which members of the community have different structures and duties.

28 Coleoptera (beetles: wood worms, weevils). This widely distributed group of nearly 300,000

species are not closely related to any other insects. They all have the fore wings modified into hard wing cases to protect the membranous hind wings and abdomen. They range tremendously in size from the feather-wing beetles less than 0·02 in (0·5 mm) long, to the Goliath and Hercules beetles which are 8 million times as bulky and up to 6 in (15 cm) long. Most live hidden in soil and under vegetation, many having lost the power of flight, but there are many well known brightly coloured garden species.

29 Strepsiptera. This small group of peculiar insects are seldom seen. They are parasites of Homoptera and Hymenoptera. The female, which is little more than a sac of developing eggs, never leaves the host, but the male can fly. Only the hind wings are developed, the fore wings being reduced to knobs like the halteres of Diptera.

Right: A beetle of the weevil family, with its long 'beak' or proboscis. Weevils are the largest family in the Animal Kingdom, with over 35,000 species. They are widely distributed and feed mainly on seeds and grain. Many are serious pests; the Cotton ball weevil causes hundreds of millions of dollars worth of damage annually in the United States.

Classification of beetles. The suborder Polyphaga contains 90% of all beetles. The Adephaga are mainly carnivorous land and water beetles. There are another two very small suborders, one of which includes the most primitive family (Cupedidae) which were the dominant beetles in the Permian, 200 million years ago.

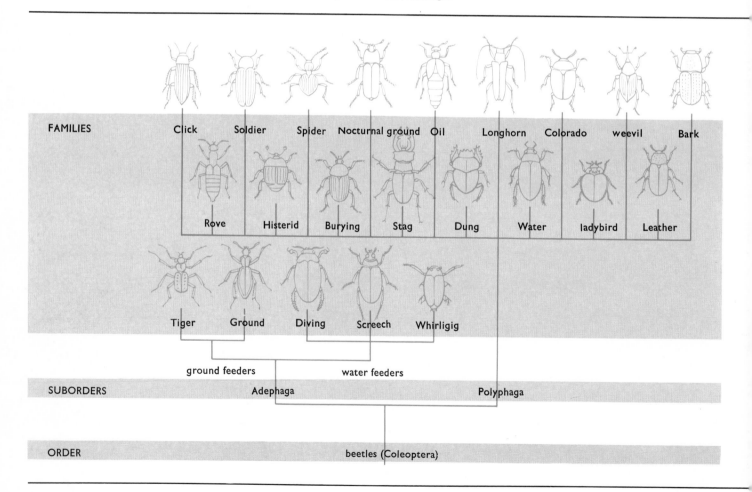

FAMILIES

Click   Soldier   Spider   Nocturnal ground   Oil   Longhorn   Colorado   weevil   Bark

Rove   Histerid   Burying   Stag   Dung   Water   ladybird   Leather

Tiger   Ground   Diving   Screech   Whirligig

ground feeders   water feeders

SUBORDERS   Adephaga   Polyphaga

ORDER   beetles (Coleoptera)

24

Basic Problems of Life

Insects are predominantly terrestrial animals. In achieving this status they have, in the course of their evolution, had to develop methods of overcoming the rigours of the inhospitable terrestrial environment. Life on this planet originated in water and the vital life-processes of all living cells today take place in an aquatic medium. An organism pursuing a life on land must maintain the aquatic environment around its cells and isolate them from the drying air. But each cell requires oxygen from the air to sustain its life, so the isolation must not be complete. Life on land subjects organisms to much greater and more frequent variations in temperature than those experienced in an aquatic environment, so the land animal must develop means, physiological or behavioural, of stabilizing its temperature. Let us see then how the insects have attempted to overcome these problems and what further limitations the solutions have imposed.

Insulation against Water Loss. Water loss from a damp body is chiefly the result of evaporation from its surface. The smaller a body is, the greater its surface area compared with its volume, that is, the greater the opportunity for water loss compared with the amount of water it contains. Since insects are rather small animals, the problem is an acute one for them and they have been obliged to develop a water-proof outer covering.

Some semi-terrestrial animals, like worms and slugs protect their body surface with a layer of slime or mucus, produced by epidermal cells on the surface of their bodies. Mucus is a compound of protein and sugar, and insect epidermal cells secrete a chemically similar material. In this case, however,

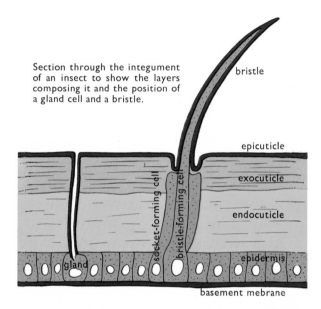

Section through the integument of an insect to show the layers composing it and the position of a gland cell and a bristle.

bristle
epicuticle
exocuticle
endocuticle
epidermis
socket-forming cell
bristle-forming cell
gland
basement mebrane

Section through the cuticle of an insect to show the layers composing it and the position of a gland cell and a bristle. The material of the cuticle is secreted by the epidermal cells whose activity is modified in the region of the bristle to form the different structures needed there.

the carbohydrate equivalent to the sugar of mucus consists of long chains of molecules of the nitrogen-containing sugar glucosamine, linked together to form a tough fibrous polymer called chitin. The chitin and protein together form the tough flexible outer skin or cuticle of the insect.

The chitin/protein complex forms the basis of the cuticular covering of insects and its tough but flexible nature makes it an ideal material to form the joints where one section of the body bends over another: however, over much of the body, where movement is not essential, the cuticle undergoes a process called tanning after it has been secreted by the epidermis. Tanning is a complex process in

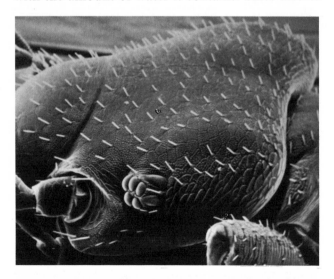

This stereoscan photograph of the head of a booklouse *Liposcelis bostrychophilus* shows the outer layer of cuticle in minute detail. The base of an antenna and a compound eye, with only seven facets, are clearly seen. The general surface is covered with minute bristles and is variously sculptured.

The male Emperor moth *Saturnia pavonia* illustrates the extent to which the plastic material of the cuticle can be moulded into elaborate shapes. The feathery antennae bear thousands of minute and intricate organs of smell and the thousands of wing scales and body hairs are all moulded to a precise pattern.

which chemicals called quinones react with the protein chains in the cuticle to link them together. The protein thus becomes a cross-linked plastic called sclerotin which is hard and very resistant to attack by chemicals. By some miraculous mechanism of control, this tanning does not occur in the region of joints, in which the cuticle remains flexible. However, the edges of the joint may be hardened and thickened so as to determine and limit the amount and direction of movement possible, thus reducing the number of muscles needed to control the movement.

Like most plastics, sclerotin is readily moulded into complex shapes, such as the numerous hairs and sense organs, the scales on butterfly wings and the complex striations on the wing cases or elytra of some beetles which give rise to beautiful iridescent colours. Similarly, on a larger scale, the legs, wings, mouthparts, intricately interlocking sexual appendages, and even the general body form itself, are all moulded in the soft cuticle laid down by epidermal cells which have themselves assumed the appropriate shape and size. Then, by the release of enzymes, or catalysts, the soft cuticle is tanned and converted to the hard sclerotin.

We get some idea of just how hard sclerotin can be when it is fully tanned from an investigation of what is often the hardest part of an insect – its jaws or mandibles. It has been found that some wood-boring beetles can bite through sheets of lead, silver, copper or zinc so the sclerotin of the mandibles must be harder than these metals.

Despite the obvious useful properties of the cuticle so far described, neither the chitin nor the sclerotin is particularly waterproof. The real waterproofing coat is a very thin layer on the surface of the cuticle. This so-called epicuticle is less than a thousandth of a millimetre thick but, even so, consists of several layers of different materials. One of these consists of wax molecules, and it is these that prevent the passage of water to the outside. In fact the most effective part of the wax barrier is a layer of long wax molecules packed together like matches in a box but standing upright. The wax molecules are packed so tightly together that water molecules cannot squeeze through the gaps between them. This precise orientation would never withstand the wear and tear suffered by the surface of the cuticle so it is covered over with a layer of randomly orientated wax molecules followed by a layer of 'cement'. Even so, the wax layer is constantly being renewed by secretion of new wax from the cells underneath. How the insect orientates the wax molecules so precisely is a complete mystery.

It is rather surprising that such a small part of the cuticle is actually concerned with water loss. In fact the hard, thick sclerotin of the wing cases of some beetles is fairly impermeable to water, but even these insects rely on the epicuticle overlying the necessarily thinner cuticle of joints to prevent desiccation. The soft white caterpillar of the clothes moth *Tineola* can live for long periods in dry furs or clothes and is therefore, despite its thin cuticle, very resistant to drying. But if this, or any other caterpillar, is allowed to crawl through material which has been dusted with silica or aluminium dust, it will

27

A Hawk-moth caterpillar in the process of devouring a leaf of its host plant. Leaves on the underside of the twig have already gone. Nine spiracles may be seen as a row of brown dots along the side of the caterpillar. From these openings, the air tubes, or trachae, enter inwards to all parts of the body.

shrivel and die within hours. The dust acts as an abrasive and disrupts the epicuticular layer so exposing the insect to desiccation. This method of combating insect pests was known to the Romans as a precaution against grain weevils and, in parts of the world today, road dust or other abrasive powders are mixed with stored grain.

This sort of abrasion is also inflicted by soil particles on many of the soft-bodied larvae of beetles, moths, flies and others which inhabit the soil. They are able to survive without becoming desiccated because the air in the soil spaces is usually more or less saturated with water vapour. If these larvae are brought into a dry situation they soon shrivel and die, but if they are taken immediately after moulting, before the new cuticle has been exposed to the abrasive effect of the soil, then they can resist desiccation as well as any other insect.

Respiration in Terrestrial Insects. A distinct disadvantage related to the impermeability of the cuticle to water is that it is also impermeable to oxygen.

Terrestrial insects obtain their oxygen from the air and use it to oxidize the sugars and fats from their food to provide the energy for muscular movement. But before the oxygen can enter their cells it must get inside the cuticle then dissolve in water before diffusing through their walls. Many of the primitive springtails have never developed a waterproof layer in their cuticle and, living a fairly inactive life in moist situations, can get enough oxygen by diffusion through their permeable cuticle, from that which is dissolved in soil water. All other insects, however, have developed a respiratory system which conveys air in a controlled manner through special openings in the cuticle.

The openings in the cuticle, called spiracles, are very small and occur laterally, one pair per segment, on parts of the abdomen and thorax. From each spiracle, the epidermis is continued inwards to form a small, branching tube whose walls are lined with cuticle which is shed at each moult. The cuticular walls of these tubes, or tracheae, are strengthened by

28

rings or spirals of cuticle like the wire support in the flexible tube of a vacuum cleaner. This strengthening prevents the collapse of the tracheae and allows them to carry air deep into the body of the insect. The tubes branch and ramify through the tissues getting ever finer like the branches of a tree till finally each branch ends with its very thin and permeable walls actually penetrating the cells of muscles and other tissues. It is here that gases dissolve in the small amount of fluid in the end of each tube. Thus oxygen from the air diffuses in to oxidize the fuels in respiration and the carbon dioxide, produced as a waste product, diffuses out to be released into the surrounding air.

In many Apterygota, the tracheae from each spiracle form a series of unconnected tufts, but in most insects, tracheae from adjacent spiracles unite to form several longitudinal trunks running the length of the body. The distribution and abundance of tracheae reflects the demand for oxygen by different tissues, thus the brain and flight muscles are well supplied. The distribution, however, may change during the development of an insect. Cells in a region of oxygen deficient tissue may extend cytoplasmic threads to contact the nearest branches of the tracheal system. The threads then contract, drawing the tracheal tubes towards the site of deficiency where new branches grow.

Movement of air through the finer tubes occurs by diffusion, but in the longer tubes a system of ventilation, similar to our breathing, occurs. Muscles in the abdomen alternately extend and compress it, the segments moving over each other telescopi-

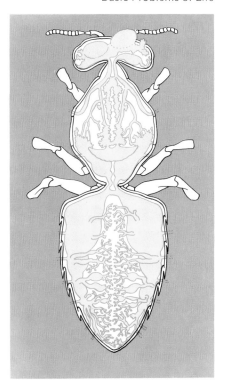

Diagram showing the air-sacs in a worker honeybee. The air-sacs are interconnected by tracheae which also communicate with the exterior via the spiracles. The numerous, minute branches of tracheae which ramify the tissues are not shown in this diagram.

cally. The changes in internal pressure force air in and out of the tracheal system. Most of the tracheae do not readily change shape or size but they are dilated in places to form thin-walled air-sacs which collapse and expand as the insect breathes. The air-sacs are often very numerous and can in some cases occupy almost half the body volume.

Thus the tracheal system allows the insect to take in oxygen and give out carbon dioxide, yet to have at the same time a surface impermeable to water. But, if air can get in through the spiracles, water vapour can get out. To minimize this effect, each spiracle is equipped with a valve – a tiny cuticular trapdoor opened by a special muscle or an elastic spring and held shut most of the time by another muscle. Except during violent exercise, each spiracle valve is normally shut and only opens when an exchange of gases is necessary. Opening is controlled either by nerve impulses, or by the direct action on the muscles of lack of oxygen and surplus carbon dioxide.

During vigorous exercise the rate of ventilation is increased, the spiracles stay open longer and, in some insects they may open at different times during the breathing sequence so causing a flow of air through the body from one end to the other. The most vigorous exercise of all is flight and here the rate of ventilation keeps pace very neatly with the flight activity. The considerable distortion of the

A Tse-tse fly *Glossina* resting on the skin of the human host after feeding. The insect's abdomen is distended by the blood meal and the host's skin bears the mark where the proboscis was inserted. Openings to the air tubes, the spiracles, occur laterally on each segment of the abdomen.

thorax caused by the flight muscles acts as a pump to drive air in and out of the thoracic air-sacs. The more active the flight, the more active the ventilation.

On the other hand, insects like the overwintering pupae of butterflies and moths, which lie dormant for months on end, need very little oxygen, and they have virtually no way of replacing lost water. The spiracles are so tightly shut that a partial vacuum develops in the tracheal system as oxygen is used up and carbon dioxide dissolves in the body fluid. Periodically the spiracles open very slightly and the partial vacuum causes air to rush in with very little loss of water. A proper opening of the spiracles to get rid of carbon dioxide may only occur three or four times a day and the loss of water is adequately compensated by the formation of 'water of metabolism' (see below). This sparse and intermittent type of ventilation does not occur in pupae living in a

Pupae of the Violet ground beetle. The immature stages of many beetles, moths and flies are soft-bodied and live in soil. Although abrasion by soil particles destroys their waterproofing layer the dampness of the soil prevents them from becoming dessicated.

moist environment and, in some insects, the extent of its occurrence is correlated with the dryness of the environment. The effectiveness of this technique in terms of conservation of water is such that it allows the small Eggar moth *Eriogaster lanestris* to remain in the pupal state for as long as seven years before emerging as an adult.

Respiration in Aquatic and Other Insects. The majority of aquatic insects obtain their oxygen directly from the air but others utilize oxygen dissolved in the water, just as fish do. The major problems facing insects which come to the surface to obtain oxygen are, to break the surface film when they get there, and to prevent water flooding their tracheal system when they dive again. Often 'hairs' around the spiracles are not readily wetted, so that they close over as the insect dives but open on the surface of the water, being spread out by surface

tension. Sometimes, as in some mosquito larvae, only the posterior spiracles function and are carried on a stalk called a siphon. When the insect surfaces to breathe, only the top of the siphon penetrates the surface and the insect remains largely submerged, suspended from the surface film. The larvae of hover flies *Eristalis* are about 0·4 in (1 cm) long and are known as the 'rat-tailed maggots'. They get this unlikely name from the fact that their siphons are telescopic and can be extended to 2·4 in (6 cm) allowing the spiracles to reach the surface while the larvae lie concealed in the mud at the bottom of the pond.

The mosquito larvae can only remain submerged while the air in the tracheal system lasts, but some insects take a surplus air store down with them in the form of a bubble of air carried in various places on the body. The giant diving beetle *Dytiscus* carries its store beneath the elytra while in *Notonecta* air is also trapped by bristles on the ventral surface of the body. As oxygen in the air bubble is used up, its concentration becomes less than that in the surrounding water and more oxygen diffuses in. The amount of oxygen available to the insect is more than was present in the original bubble which is thus acting as a gill.

Some insects have specialized in using this principle to obtain their oxygen from the water. Very numerous, small hairs trap a thin layer of air, called a plastron, over much of the surface of the body. This forms a large surface area for the exchange of

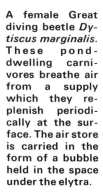

A female Great diving beetle *Dytiscus marginalis*. These pond-dwelling carnivores breathe air from a supply which they replenish periodically at the surface. The air store is carried in the form of a bubble held in the space under the elytra.

A pupa and three larvae of the mosquito *Culex pipiens* suspended from the surface film through which their breathing tubes protrude. In the larvae only the posterior spiracles function and are carried on a stalk called a siphon.

gases with the water. In the aquatic bug *Aphel-ocheirus*, there are about 2·5 million hairs per square millimetre and they can withstand a pressure of four atmospheres, so the plastron would only collapse at excessive depths.

In some very small larvae, such as first instar larvae of the dipteran midge *Chironomus*, the diffusion of oxygen from the water through the thin cuticle is adequate. A few such larvae are unique among insects in having haemoglobin in their blood. This, of course, is the respiratory pigment, common in vertebrates, which has special properties making it ideal as an oxygen carrier. However, in general, blood circulation is poor in insects and the rate of

diffusion of oxygen through the blood is too slow to meet the oxygen requirements of larger insects.

Thus the majority of insects which obtain their oxygen from water have a closed tracheal system, with no functional spiracles. Oxygen diffuses through the cuticle into the tracheal system where, as a gas, it diffuses much more rapidly around the body than it could do if dissolved in liquid. In larvae of the black fly *Simulium*, there is a network of fine tracheae immediately under the general body cuticle, but usually there are leaf-like extensions of the body having thin cuticle and a tracheal network. These 'tracheal gills' occur in various positions; in damselfly larvae there are three such gills at the tail

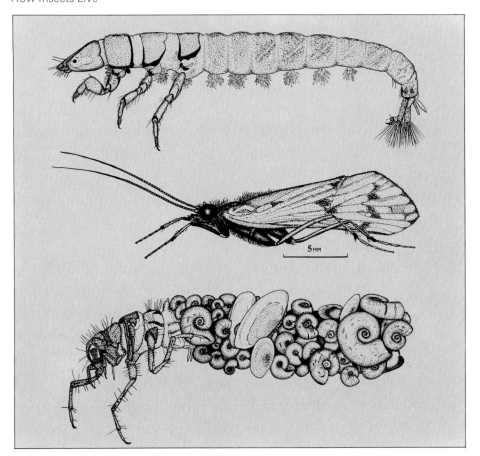

The larva of the Caddis fly *Hydropsyche* (top) showing tufts of gills on thorax and abdomen. The centre drawing shows the adult Caddis fly *Phryganea obsoleta*. The bottom drawing shows a larva of *Limnophilus centralis* emerging from its case of tiny Water snail shells.

5MM

end whilst caddis fly larvae have filamentous abdominal gills. A flow of water is maintained over the gills to prevent the accumulation of 'spent' water around them and the gills often move like fans. The gills of larval dragonflies occur inside the rectum and water is drawn in and out over them by muscular pumping of the abdomen.

Some insects obtain oxygen by thrusting their spiracles into the air-spaces in aquatic plant stems. This usually occurs in those larvae of true flies (Diptera) and beetles (Coleoptera) which live in mud containing very little oxygen. In the larva of the mosquito *Mansonia*, the functional spiracle at the end of the abdomen is at the top of a sharp-pointed, conical siphon. The toothed surface of this siphon is used to rasp a hole in the plant tissue.

The pupae of many Diptera and of some Coleoptera occur in aquatic habitats which are subject to drying up. Since the pupae are unable to move to a more suitable environment, they must be equipped to breathe in both water and air. This they do by means of spiracular gills. These are extensions of the spiracle, or the cuticle around it, to form a long hollow process opening to the outside through small holes. The gill bears a plastron surface which is used

in water, while in air the small holes provide an entry for oxygen but limit the water loss from the developing adult insect inside.

Parasitic insects which live inside the body of their hosts obtain oxygen from the host tissues by diffusion through their own thin cuticle. Additionally, the posterior spiracles of the parasite may penetrate the tracheal supply or penetrate the body wall of the host. This occurs in many tachinid larvae (Diptera) which parasitize other insects, whereas the larvae of *Melinda*, another dipteran, which parasitizes snails, sticks its posterior spiracles out through the respiratory opening of the snail.

Parasites of vertebrates also often use atmospheric air but not so the larvae of the dipteran *Gasterophilus*, which lives in the stomach of the horse. Here it only encounters air intermittently in bubbles with the food. The oxygen absorbed is stored by haemoglobin, associated with the tracheal system, to be used during the periods when no air is available.

Control of the Chemical Environment. To function effectively, living cells must be bathed in a fluid of fairly constant composition. The blood system plays a part in the maintenance of this equilibrium by transporting and distributing salts, hormones, the products of digestion and metabolism and by its possession of a system of chemicals which ensures that the acidity of the blood remains relatively constant. It plays some part too, in the maintenance of salt and water balance in the body but this is mainly achieved by the Malpighian tubules and the rectum as we shall see.

Insects have an open blood system in which the blood is not confined to vessels but circulates among the organs, propelled by the action of a longitudinal heart on the dorsal or upper side of the body. This, the only blood vessel, is a tube situated above the gut and extending through the thorax and abdomen. The posterior part is the heart and it is divided by valves into a series of chambers, while the anterior part is the dorsal aorta. The heart is cut off from the rest of the body cavity by a muscular diaphragm. When the heart is relaxed, blood enters through lateral openings in the diaphragm and, on contraction, is forced forward through the series of valves to be delivered from the aorta which opens in the head. With the aid of undulatory movements of the diaphragm, and other pulsatile structures, the blood is circulated throughout the general body cavity and appendages. The action of the heart may

be under nervous or hormonal control but sometimes the control apparently resides within the heart itself.

The blood or haemolymph of insects consists of a fluid plasma in which cells are suspended. The plasma acts as a lubricant and a system for the transport of materials around the body. It is usually yellowish or greenish in colour except in those few midge larvae which have haemoglobin of the usual red colour. The plasma may act as a store of substances like sugars and proteins and it is of course an important reservoir of water. The hydrostatic pressure of the blood is important in locomotion in soft-bodied larvae and in expansion of the body after moulting. The blood cells are involved in protection of the body in various ways. Some actually ingest foreign particles of various sorts, bacteria and cell debris, while others build up layers around an invader which is too big to be ingested. This reaction may inhibit the activities of an internal parasite. Some blood cells can react with poisonous substances to render them harmless and one of their most important functions is to accumulate at sites of injury where they cause coagulation, attack germs and generally promote healing.

Since the blood bathes the tissues and cells of the

The European water scorpion *Nepa* having captured a small fish with the front pair of legs which look like a scorpion's claws. The slender 'tail' is a breathing tube which the aquatic bug pushes up through the surface film to take in air.

body, it largely determines the nature of the internal environment and it is the job of the excretory system to maintain the uniformity of the blood. The principle organs involved are the Malpighian tubules, named after their discoverer, Marcello Malpighi, a seventeenth century Italian scientist. The long narrow blind-ending tubules open into the front of the hindgut. They often have muscle strands in their walls enabling them to writhe in the blood, so increasing their ability to absorb water, salts and

Mealworms, the larvae of a beetle *Tenebrio molitor*, a pest of flour mills, can live in very dry conditions. These larvae are better known as food for caged birds and other pets.

excretory products from it. This mixture then passes through the rectum along with undigested food material. In the walls of the rectum there are special cells which can reabsorb salts and water according to the requirements of the insect. We get rid of most of our nitrogenous waste in the urine in the form of urea which is very soluble and needs a lot of water to flush it out. But in insects, where conservation of water is important, the nitrogenous waste is uric acid which is almost insoluble and takes very little water with it. The drier the conditions under which the insect lives, the more efficient is the reabsorption of water by the rectum.

Control of the Physical Environment. Some features of the physical environment, such as daylength, may be of profound significance to certain insects but are not modified or controlled. Again humidity may be a factor of vital importance and, in general, insects utilize their small size and their mobility to select areas, micro-habitats, in which the humidity conditions are favourable or, alternatively, they postpone their excursions until the humidity is suitable. Thus biting midges are active in

some localities during the morning and evening but may attack with equal vigour at mid-day on humid days. So far as temperature is concerned, however, insects appear to have developed more adequate means of counteracting the variations which occur, especially in temperate regions.

While birds and mammals can maintain their body temperatures within quite close limits, insects do not have such a sophisticated mechanism but are by no means limited to the temperature of their surroundings. Many insects can raise their body temperature by fluttering their wings without flying. This utilizes the metabolic heat generated by the flight muscles. This behaviour usually occurs if the insects are disturbed at temperatures too low for flight: the highly efficient flight muscles cannot develop full power until they have 'warmed up' to about 79°F (26°C) but some flight is possible at lower temperatures than that. The moth *Saturnia* can increase its body temperature in this way to 96°F

The Gatekeeper butterfly *Epiphele tithonus* feeding on a flower of the rose family. This common British butterfly is often seen during the summer when its activity is closely regulated by the sun. Even on warm days it stops flying when clouds pass in front of the sun but starts again when the sun comes out.

The Privet hawk-moth *Sphinx liqustri* resting on a tree trunk. The hairs and scales which give this insect its beautiful markings serve an additional purpose. They form an efficient insulating layer which helps to keep the insect's body warmer than the surrounding air. In cool climates this is necessary for efficient flight.

(36°C) at an air temperature of 64°F (18°C). The large beetle *Geotrupes* employs this technique with remarkable efficiency; the wing muscles are contracted isometrically without movement of the wings.

Alternatively some insects rely entirely on radiant heat from the sun to keep their bodies at an active temperature. Even on warm summer days, the Gatekeeper butterfly *Epinephele tithonus* disappears when the sun goes in but can fly again a few minutes after it comes out. Locusts and grasshoppers have mastered the art of behavioural temperature regulation. In the low temperatures of early morning, the locust turns broadside on to the sun and leans over, even spreading its legs, to expose the maximum possible body area to the sun's radiation. At the other extreme, in the heat of the day, it turns to face the sun, exposing a smaller surface, and raises the body off the ground, permitting a free circulation of air and avoiding the excessive temperatures at the surface of the ground. In a larval locust, the ratio of the surfaces exposed in these two positions, 'flanking' and 'facing', is 6:1. If ground tempera-

tures become excessive the locust climbs into the vegetation where it may be shaded and stands side on to the wind so increasing evaporative cooling. In the evening, as the temperature falls, the locust crouches close to the warm ground, gaining heat by conduction. These behavioural responses of warming and cooling enable the locust to keep its body temperature between 95°F (35°C) and 105°F (41°C) for as long as possible.

Since it is particularly important for an insect to keep its flight motor warm it is not surprising to find that the thorax has an insulated covering. Thus the hairs on bees and flies, and the scales on butterflies and moths, serve to insulate the body. The Privet hawk-moth *Sphinx ligustri* can raise its body temperature 30°F (17°C) above the surrounding air, but with its thorax shaved of scales and hair it can only achieve an excess temperature of about 14°F (8°C). It might be thought that a dragonfly with its bare and shining thorax would be badly insulated, but this is not so. It insulates its flight muscles with a covering of air-sacs just underneath the cuticle of the thorax.

35

A number of insects, particularly overwintering larvae and pupae can withstand freezing temperatures with no ill effects. Death due to low temperatures results from the formation of ice crystals in the tissues. Often, glycerol appears in the bloodstream of insects before they hibernate. This amounts to about 3% in the Giant silkmoth *Hyalophora cecropia* but can be as much as 20% in a parasitic hymenopteran of Western Canada, *Bracon cephi*. The glycerol may lower the freezing point of the blood to about 14°F (−15°C) but other, unknown factors reduce the actual freezing point much further.

Some remarkable feats of survival are recorded in insects which commonly encounter very adverse circumstances and withstand them by allowing the water in their bodies to evaporate. The larva of the chironomid midge *Polypedilum* lives in rock pools in West Africa. When the pools dry up, it loses its own body water and can survive for years in a shrivelled up state in the mud until rain fills the pools again. When this happens, the larvae soon swell up and within half an hour they are moving about and feeding again. In the dehydrated state they have recovered completely after being kept at the temperature of boiling water 212°F (100°C) for one minute or in liquid air at −284°F (−190°C) for three days.

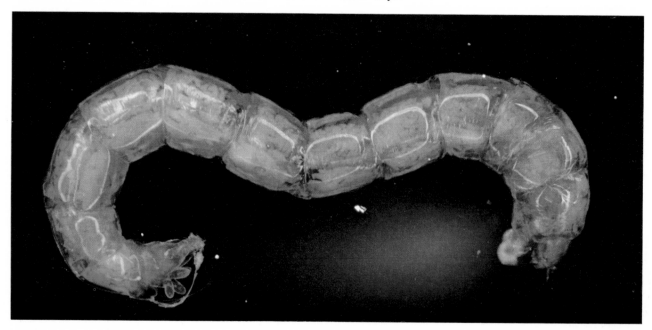

A larva of the family Chironomidae. The early instars of these small, aquatic larvae obtain their oxygen from the water in which they live by diffusion through the thin cuticle all over the body. A few species, like this one, are red in colour and are unique among insects in having haemoglobin in their blood. This red pigment common in vertebrates has special properties making it a very effective oxygen carrier. It takes up oxygen readily where oxygen is plentiful, in the water, and releases it readily where it is scarce, in the insect's tissues.

Locomotion on Land and Water

The ability to move from place to place at some stage in the life history is an important attribute of all animals, and locomotor abilities are well developed in insects. The great mobility of insects, conferred by the power of flight, contributes largely to their success, but walking and swimming in the pursuit of food and mates, and in escaping from danger, are also very important.

There are three basic systems required for effective locomotion: a sensory system reporting on conditions in, on and around the body; a central nervous system to identify, interpret and co-ordinate that information; a system of muscles, controlled by the nervous system and capable of producing the required movements. Most commonly, legs are used to propel the insect on land or in water and the legs are moved by the pull of muscles attached to the rigid, cuticular skeleton. Where a rigid skeleton is not available, as in soft-bodied larvae, the muscles act against a hydrostatic skeleton provided by the pressure of haemolymph in the body, and produce a locomotory movement called crawling.

Crawling. The basic movement involved in crawl-ing is a forward extension of the front part of the body which then takes a new grip on the substratum while the back end is drawn forward. This movement is achieved by the action of muscles on the soft, fluid-filled body. Although the cuticle is soft, it is essential as an external skeleton. If the cuticle is punctured, the internal fluid escapes: the body of, for example, a caterpillar becomes limp and loco-motion is no longer possible. The body wall of caterpillars is lined by a network of so-called turgor muscles which do not themselves cause movement but keep up a steady pressure on the haemolymph to keep the body turgid. Since fluid is incompressible, if the body is contracted in one region, it must be extended in another by an equal amount. In prac-tice, these contractions and expansions are con-trolled by muscles involved in locomotion in such a way that progression is achieved.

In addition to the normal three pairs of thoracic legs, caterpillars have up to four pairs of 'false' legs on segments three to six of the abdomen, together with a pair of anal claspers. Each false leg has suckers and hooks on the 'foot', and the cavity inside them, the lumen, is continous with the haemolymph.

  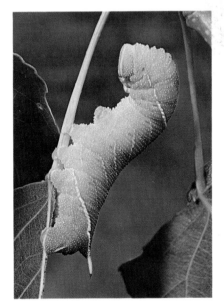

Left: A caterpillar of the Eyed hawkmoth *Smerinthus ocellatus*. The soft-skinned fluid-filled body is kept in a firm and turgid state by the constant contraction of muscles lining the body wall. Centre: A Looper caterpillar which has false legs only on segments six and ten of the abdomen. Right: The Lobster moth caterpillar *Stauropus fagi*. Its false legs are clearly seen here gripping the twigs.

The caterpillar of the Atlas moth *Attacus atlas* here demonstrates all the legs it uses in crawling. Behind the head at the top of the picture are the three pairs of thoracic legs then, further back, are the four pairs of much larger false legs, and finally the pair of claspers at the tip of the abdomen.

Below: Movements occurring during crawling in a caterpillar. Contraction of the dorsal longitudinal muscle (1) in segment III moves that segment forward, while contraction of vertical muscles (2) in segment IV lifts its false leg (3). Ventral longitudinal muscles (4) in segment V then contract to move its false leg forwards and increase of haemolymph pressure extends the leg to take a new grip. These waves of movement pass forwards to produce forward locomotion.

Crawling is carried out mainly by these legs and waves of movement start at the back and pass forwards, at least three segments being in different stages of contraction at any one time. The dorsal longitudinal muscles move one segment forward while the vertical muscles lift up the false leg of the segment behind and the ventral longitudinal muscles move the false leg forward in the segment behind that. When their forward step has been completed, each pair of false legs is then inflated by the pressure of haemolymph and the feet extended to take a new grip.

Geometrid, or earth-measuring, caterpillars have false legs only on abdominal segments six and ten and have a slightly modified mode of progression. The thoracic legs release their grip, the front end of the caterpillar stretches forward to take a new grip and the hind end is then looped up behind the thorax to start the sequence again. Similar mechanisms operate in the legless larvae of Diptera where adhesion is aided by rows of hooks on the underside of some segments. Sometimes, as in larvae of the housefly *Musca*, the hooked mandibles are used to achieve anchorage.

Walking. The most common mode of progression used by insects is walking by means of six thoracic legs. It is thought that the ancestors of insects had more than six legs but as the legs became longer to facilitate faster running, they became fewer to reduce problems of co-ordination and six is the minimum number for great stability over a wide range of speeds. Functional efficiency is increased by having the bases of the legs close together and near the head. Hence the insect thorax was evolved and, as wings developed in this region too, it became the locomotor centre of the insect.

The pattern of movement of the insect's legs is quite complex and, of course, is normally executed

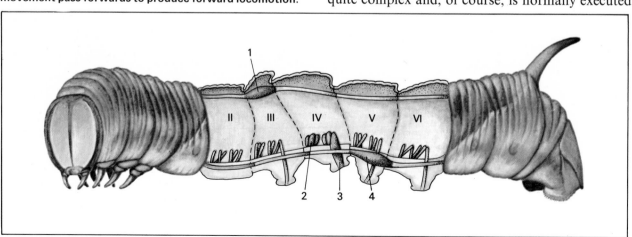

The Giant West Indian bush-cricket *Nesonotus denticulatus*. The various sections of a typical walking leg are shown here. On the underside of the foot are broad pads which aid in gripping smooth surfaces and right at the tip is a pair of claws which grip in minute crevices.

by the action of attached muscles. These claws take a remarkably firm grip even on surfaces which to us appear quite smooth, but whose imperfections are sufficiently coarse for the tiny claws to grip. The other device which enables many insects to obtain a grip on really smooth surfaces is a soft pad which lies between the claws. The undersurface of this pad is variously ridged and probably maintains its grip on smooth surfaces by virtue of a very thin oily film on its surface. The pad readily slides over the surface in one direction, but in the other direction, the tips of the sloping ridges cut through the film and come into such intimate contact with the substrate that adhesion occurs. As an insect uses these pads to walk on a window pane, it pulls each foot inwards towards the centre of its body so maintaining the adhesion, but when this tension is removed, the pad

very rapidly so that it is difficult to follow by eye. If, however, the motion is filmed and the film viewed at a much slower speed, the various patterns associated with different circumstances emerge. To simplify, the insect supports its weight on the first and third legs of one side and the second leg of the opposite side, while the remaining three legs step forward in unison. These three legs then take the weight while the other three step forward, so the insect proceeds by stepping with alternating triangles of support. This 'tripod' gait is very stable, as the centre of gravity always lies within the triangle made by the feet and the insect can stop at any point in its stepping sequence without toppling over.

The role played by individual legs is no less complex than the total pattern of movement they produce. The legs act as struts propping up the weight of the body and also as levers magnifying the movements which the thoracic muscles apply to their bases. Other muscles inside the legs can be used to extend or flex the legs. Thus a leg stretched out in front of the insect can be flexed to pull the insect forward onto it, then, as the body passes over it, it can be extended so as to push the body further forward. Combine all these effects and you have a very complex and carefully controlled set of activities occurring in each leg.

In the course of walking, the power used to move the insect is conveyed via the legs and applied to the ground. It is essential, therefore, that the feet of the insect obtain a firm grip on the ground, and to this end two devices are commonly used. On the last segment of the tarsus is a pair of downward curved claws whose sharp points can be dug into the ground

The foot of a fly seen from underneath. The last segment of the tarsus bears a pair of downward curved claws. Their black colour indicates that they are heavily sclerotized and therefore very hard. There are muscles attached to the claws so that they may be dug into the ground and can in fact take a grip on surfaces which appear to be quite smooth.

A Grasshopper showing the powerful modification of the hind legs for jumping. The broad femur contains the main muscles arranged in rows and all pulling on a central tendon. The 'herring-bone' pattern on the femur reveals the arrangement of the muscles inside. The sharp spines on the hind tibia are used in defence.

is easily detached to make the next forward step.

The co-ordination of the complex process of walking occurs at several levels; there is co-ordination of the movements of different parts of a single leg, there is co-ordination between the legs on opposite sides of a segment so that they step alternately, and there is co-ordination of the stepping activity of the three segments of the thorax. A prerequisite for this control is that the insect should have an adequate awareness of the position and activity of all of its limbs at any one moment. This information is provided by a system of sensory receptors in each leg which monitor such parameters as the angle between joints (by hair beds), the tension developed in muscles (by stretch receptors) and stresses (by campaniform sensilla) occurring in the cuticle such as those produced when the leg is bearing the weight of the insect. These different types of receptors are described more fully later. The information from these receptors is fed initially to that part of the central nervous system contained within the segment to which the leg is attached. The nervous control of the leg muscles derives from the same area and it is conceivable that the control of stepping could be self-contained within a segment. Indeed, evidence suggests that pressure on the

underside of the foot causes the leg to be pushed down, and pressure on top of the foot causes it to be raised. Further, activity in the muscles which raise the leg results in suppression of activity in those muscles which lower it and the same sort of reflex inhibition exists between legs on opposite sides of a segment. It has been suggested that once walking is initiated, the changes in weight distribution and in drag forces are themselves enough to maintain walking by reflex reaction without the need for central co-ordination, that is, each step is the direct stimulation for the next. The situation depicted is like that of two men in a pantomime horse, in which the two pairs of legs are rather imperfectly in touch with each other.

Some further observations indicate that this is not the whole story. For example, holding one leg still, and therefore altering the feedback from it, often does not interfere with the gait of the other legs. An insect suspended in the air will 'walk' with a normal gait on a ball of pith which it holds with its feet. Here the weight of the ball pulls down on the feet instead of the weight of the insect pushing down on them. There is now good evidence that the central nervous system of each segment has its own oscillator, producing an alternating output which controls the stepping of the legs of that segment. The rate of movement and the fine control of stepping relies on the sensory feedback to modify the central output, and feedback between segments ensures that the three segments remain in synchrony with each other. The sophistication of this control is indicated by the fact that if one or more legs are lost, the pattern of movement is quickly changed to the one which best fits the new situation.

Jumping. Jumping is usually an escape reaction but some Orthoptera such as grasshoppers augment their normal walking progression with short hops. It is normally the hind legs which are modified to provide the power for the jump. Thus in Orthoptera the upper part, or femur, of each hind leg is much enlarged to house rows of muscles all pulling on a central tendon attached to the lower part, or tibia. In a fifth instar *Locusta* a force of 28 oz (800 gm) is exerted on the head of the tibia. The lever effect of the tibia reduces the thrust on the ground from each hind foot to about 0·7 oz (20 gm) but this is still quite adequate to launch the insect, weighing only 0·05 oz (1·5 gm), rapidly into the air. As a corollary to reduction of thrust, the rate of movement is increased by the lever effect, giving the locust a take-off velocity of 11 ft 6 in (3·5 m) per second. This enables the fifth instar *Locusta* to achieve an escape jump 27 in (70 cm) long and 11·5 in (30 cm) high.

A technique commonly used by jumping insects is gradually to build up muscular tension then suddenly to release it, so projecting the animal into the air. In fleas (Siphonaptera) the hind leg is moved back and up above the body by a powerful muscle. The muscle continues to contract, squeezing the leg against a pad of a very elastic type of cuticle called resilin, which is compressed more and more by the pressure. The system is rather unstable and slight sideways movement of the muscle, produced by a laterally inserted muscle, causes the femur to swing rapidly downwards as the tension in the elastic pad is released. The two hind legs thus strike the ground and the flea is projected into the air. By this means, a flea can accomplish a long jump of 13 in (43 cm) and a high jump of 8 in (20 cm). To compete with this on a size for size basis, a man would have to achieve a high jump of 800 ft (250 m).

The sudden release of tension has been exploited in a number of other ways not involving legs. In the springtails (Collembola), a modified abdominal appendage is turned forwards under the abdomen and its forked tip engages on a catch on the third abdominal segment. Muscles contract to extend the

appendage and tension builds up till it suddenly slips out of the catch and the insect is projected into the air as its tail appendage straightens out – hence the common name for Collembola. The Elateridae or click beetles can right themselves when turned on their backs. The back is arched and a prong on the first thoracic segment engages in a socket on the second. The insect then attempts to straighten its back and tension builds till the prong slips out of the socket and the back suddenly straightens, hitting the ground and projecting the insect high in the air. The sudden movement is very rapid indeed; when filmed by a high-speed cine camera running at 5,000 frames per second, the whole movement is over in 2 frames of film. The subsequent passage of the insect through the air is remarkably tortuous and uncontrolled when viewed on a slowed down film and the crash-landing is spectacular.

A flea, caught on man but probably of the species characteristically living on a cat or a dog. The large and powerful hind legs project the flea into the air for its remarkable jump. The smooth, laterally flattened body facilitates crawling amongst the fur of the host.

Swimming. Most of the free-swimming insects using their legs as a means of propulsion are adult bugs (Heteroptera) or beetles (Coleoptera). Usually their bodies are smooth and streamlined and dorsoventrally flattened so that they offer minimal resistance to movement through the water. The thrust which pushes the insect through the water is provided by the hind legs, and sometimes by the middle legs as well. The two legs of a segment move together like oars in a rowing boat, as distinct from the alternating movement employed in terrestrial locomotion. As on land, the forward thrust is provided by the backward stroke, or retraction, of the legs. However, where in terrestrial locomotion, the return stroke, protraction, is achieved with the leg out of contact with the substratum, in water this is impossible and protraction tends to produce a backwards movement of the insect. The thrust produced

The Backswimmer, an aquatic bug of the family *Notonectidae*, photographed from below showing reflection in the surface film. This insect swims upside down in the water, hence its name, and uses the long hind legs, fringed with hairs, as paddles.

is proportional to the area and to the velocity of the leg so that if these are greater on retraction than protraction, forward motion of the insect is achieved.

The beetle, *Acilius*, overcomes the problem by executing a very fast back stroke and a slow forward stroke but, in general, greater reliance is placed on altering the effective area of the leg. This method is employed by the giant water beetle *Dytiscus*. The hind tibia and tarsi are flattened from front to back to form a paddle, of which the area is further increased by a fringe of stiff hairs, which are articulated at the base. During the power stroke, the leg is held straight and the hairs spread to present a maximum area. On the recovery stroke the leg bends at the joint between the femur and tibia so that the paddle trails behind and the hairs fold inwards to reduce the area further. These movements are all passive and produced by the resistance of the water: at the beginning of the power stroke, the leg and hairs are passively extended again to present their maximum area. Similarly in the whirligig beetle *Gyrinus* the segments of the hind leg are broad and flat and can be opened and closed like a fan between power and recovery strokes.

Many aquatic insects use methods other than rowing with the legs for swimming under water. In the worm-like larvae of midges (Diptera) lateral undulations, like those of a snake, propel the insect through the water. In mosquito larvae, the same technique is augmented by a fan of bristles at the end of the abdomen acting like the tail of a fish. Similarly, larval mayflies (Ephemeroptera) and damselflies (Zygoptera) swim by vertical undulations of these tail filaments. *Caraphractus cinctus* (Hymenoptera), which parasitizes the aquatic eggs of dytiscus beetles, swims jerkily under water by flapping its tiny wings.

Walking on and Under Water. The least extensive adaptations for aquatic locomotion occur in those insects which obtain oxygen from the water by means of gills or plastrons. Those insects which come to the surface to renew their air supply and submerge with a bubble of air, must swim to overcome the buoyancy their air store gives them. The gill breathers, however, have a density greater than that of water and can walk freely on the bottom. The mode of walking is essentially the same as that employed on land with some compensation being made for the resistance of the water. In the caddis fly *Trianodes* (Trichoptera) the larval case, built from plant material, has a dorsal hood which produces a certain amount of lift as it moves through the water. To compensate this, the legs pull slightly downwards when walking. In addition to walking normally on the substrate, larval anisopteran dragonflies have developed a method of jet propulsion as an escape reaction. They normally breathe by pumping water in and out of the rectum, which contains gills. When disturbed, the insect forcibly expels water backwards through the anus at a velocity of about 8 ft (2·5 m) per second and the reaction drives the larva forwards at 12–16 in (30–50 cm) per second. The legs are laid close to the body so offering a minimum of resistance to this manoeuvre.

Water has a surface film of sufficient rigidity for insects to walk on it, provided that their cuticles are sufficiently hydrofuge, or water-repellent, to prevent

them getting wet. The most familiar of insects living on the water surface are the pond skaters like *Gerris* (Heteroptera). Simultaneous movements of the long middle and hind legs are used to row the insect along the surface. The tarsi appear not to penetrate the surface but rest in depressions which they produce in the surface film. On the other hand, springtails, such as *Podura aquatica*, also have hydrofuge cuticles but the claws are wettable and penetrate the surface film, so obtaining a purchase. The ventral tube on the first abdominal segment is also wettable and anchors the insect to the water but it can escape by using its 'spring-tail' in the same way as do terrestrial Collembola.

An extraordinary device for locomotion on the

The female Great diving beetle *Dytiscus marginalis* showing the hair-fringed hind legs used in swimming. The hairs spread to increase the area on the power stroke and fold to decrease it on the recovery stroke.

surface film has been developed by some staphilinid beetles of the genus *Stenus*. They live on grass stems by mountain streams and not uncommonly fall into the water. They can walk on the surface only slowly but are often seen to glide along without apparent effort. Investigation reveals that they secrete, from glands at the tip of the abdomen, a substance which lowers the surface tension of the water behind the insect. The insect is in fact drawn forward by the normal surface tension in front of it, and can control the direction of its progress by moving its abdomen from side to side.

The Waterboatman *Notonecta glauca* hanging from the surface film through which the tips of the claws penetrate. These insects must swim actively to counteract the buoyancy of their air store. The air is trapped amongst the hairs of the ventral surface and is seen here as glistening bubbles.

Wings and Flight

The development of wings was an outstanding event in the evolution of insects. It gave them an unprecedented mobility in the pursuit of food and mates, in escaping from enemies and, perhaps most significantly, it facilitated dispersal and opened up new environmental niches for exploitation.

With the possession of a muscular thorax potentially having aerodynamic balance, the insects were, in a sense, pre-adapted for the development of flight. There is no direct evidence of how wings developed but it seems to have occurred only once in the course of evolution and although the wings of present-day insects exhibit a wide range of modifications, they are all built on the same basic plan.

Occurrence and Structure of Wings. Fully developed wings occur only in adult insects, which usually have two pairs of wings arising dorso-laterally on the second and third thoracic segments. Each wing is a hollow outpushing of cuticle forming a thin flap, supported by tubular struts called veins. In the areas between the veins, the two layers of cuticle are closely opposed, whereas each of the major veins contains a nerve, trachea and blood vessels. The main veins run from base to tip of the wing and are more numerous near the front edge which experiences most stress during flight. These longitudinal veins are braced by a few cross-veins and the vein patterns produced are numerous but very constant for each species. This has been very useful to taxonomists in enabling them to identify insects and to work out the family relationships between them.

The dragonfly *Libellula quadrimaculata* which lives north of the Arctic Circle. Dragonflies are powerful fliers despite their low wing beat frequency. They also glide well on their transparent and glistening wings.

The Silver silk or Tailed comet moth *Argema mitterei* laying eggs. This beautiful picture illustrates the form of lepidopteran wings. The scales which produce the colour patterns also smooth the air currents and increase the efficiency of the wings.

Modifications of Wings. In dragonflies (Odonata), termites (Isoptera) and scorpion flies (Mecoptera) the two pairs of wings are of more or less the same shape and size but, in other insects, one or both pairs have usually become modified from the basic form. Sometimes, as in grasshoppers (Orthoptera), the

An East African grasshopper in flight. Grasshoppers and locusts fly well and sometimes cover enormous distances. As well as active flight, these insects are capable of gliding for long distances with the fore wings locked in the outstretched position.

hind wings are much larger than the fore wings and may have additional lobes, like those of the swallow-tailed butterflies. Such projections from the hind wing take an extreme form in some lacewings (Neuroptera) where the hind wings are reduced to slender ribbons which trail out behind the insect as it flies. Alternatively, where the hind wings provide the major surface for flight, the fore wings assume a protective role. Thus in Orthoptera and earwigs

(Dermaptera) the fore wings are leathery while in beetles (Coleoptera) the fore wings, or elytra as they are called, are very heavily thickened and have lost their basic venation. Unlike most wings, when folded the elytra of beetles do not overlap, but meet in the midline where they are held together by a tongue and groove joint running along their length. In some beetles, the fore wings have fused together along the midline so that they cannot open and the hind wings have atrophied. In those cases where the fore wings are protective, the larger hind wings must be folded away under them after use. To this end, the long dark veins have paler, weaker points at which folding may occur. The technique of wing-folding has been mastered by many beetles, bugs (Hemiptera) and by earwigs. Using the tips of their abdomens to prod their wings in the required direction, staphilinid beetles fold their hind wings longitudinally, transversely and obliquely into a neat parcel to be stowed beneath the wing cases formed by the fore wings. But the real experts in wing 'origami' are the earwigs whose hind wings are closed up like a fan, then folded over twice. They are seldom seen in flight and no wonder – wing folding is too much bother!

In the bees, ants and wasps (Hymenoptera) it is the hind wings which are reduced in size and the power for flight is provided largely by the fore wings. Similarly in flies (Diptera) each hind wing is reduced

Left: The morphology of a typical beetle showing how the wings are held at rest (right) and in flight (left). The thickened, protective fore wings, or elytra, meet in the midline and the membranous hind wings are folded under them. Right: A seven-spot ladybird with wings spread in flight just after take-off. The fore wings remain more or less stationary while the hind wings produce the power for flight. When the insect leaps into the air, the loss of tarsal contact initiates flight activity.

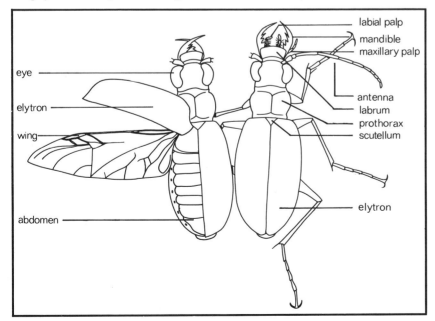
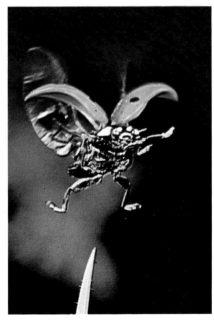

The Hover fly *Volucella* on a scabious flower. Like the housefly, they are masters of aerobatics and the arts of landing and taking off in unlikely orientations. The ability to fly forwards, backwards, sideways, upwards and downwards is essential to their way of life.

to a haltere, a stalk with a knob at the end, which acts as a sense organ enabling the fly to carry out complex manoeuvres in the air.

Sometimes both pairs of wings diverge from the basic pattern. This may occur in the interests of camouflage as in some butterflies and moths (Lepidoptera) where the irregular shape of the wings helps to break up the outline of the insect at rest. Sometimes the effective area of the wings is increased by fringes of hairs. This occurs on the plume moths whose wings are deeply lobed and fringed with hairs and also in very small insects, such as thrips (Thysanoptera) where the wings are reduced to thin straps fringed with long hairs. In some cases, both pairs of wings may be reduced or even totally absent. Winglessness may be associated with life in a habitat where wings would be a nuisance. Such is the case with lice and fleas which spend their lives crawling among the hair or feathers of their hosts. On the other hand, the Apterygotes have never developed wings and are thought to have diverged from the main stem of insect evolution before the development of wings occurred.

One further modification needs to be mentioned. Although most insects have two pairs of wings, the fore and hind wings do not operate independently of each other and greatest efficiency is achieved when the two wings on each side of the body beat together. This 'two-winged' condition is achieved by linking together the fore and hind wings on each side of the body in a number of elegant ways. One half of the coupling mechanism is on the trailing edge of the fore wing and it engages with a complementary mechanism on the leading edge of the hind wing. In some Lepidoptera coupling is achieved simply by having the edges of the two wings overlapping, which prevents them moving out of phase, but many other Lepidoptera have a stiff bristle, or group of bristles, near the base of the leading edge of the hind wing, which engages firmly with a series of similar bristles, or in some cases with a cuticular catch, on the underside of the fore wing. In Hymenoptera a row of minute hooks along the front of the hind wing catch into a fold on the back edge of the fore wing. The two wings on one side may be hooked together before the insect takes to the air, and unhooked again after it has alighted.

Gliding Flight. It is always exciting to watch the apparently erratic flight of one of the larger dragonflies as it patrols on glistening wings above a stream in search of its insect prey. Periodically the wings stop beating and are held stiffly outstretched as the insect glides for sometimes considerable distances with very little loss of height. When the dragonfly relaxes its flight muscles, the wings automatically lock in the gliding position and it is suggested that the inability of dragonflies to fold their wings is an adaptation to this, rather than a primitive feature, since wings locked in a gliding position mean that next to no effort is used in gliding. Locusts can also lock their fore wings in the outstretched position and the desert locust is a master of sustained gliding, being able to cover 8 ft (2·5 m) in still air without a single wing-stroke. Gliding is also accomplished by butterflies, in which a 'click mechanism' locks the wings in the appropriate attitude, and many other insects are able to glide for short distances.

If the air is moving, and particularly if it is moving upwards as in the thermal currents that occur on hot days, insects can utilize the same technique to soar for considerable distances without muscular effort. There is a report of a swarm of locusts which circled round and round in a thermal for six hours without ever beating their wings. By this means the desert locust can reach great altitudes and has been reported at 3,000 ft (900 m) above ground level. If the insect expends little or no effort during these feats, clearly the power used in doing the work must come from elsewhere and we shall consider next the source of that power and how it acts to produce flight.

Forces Acting on the Wings. The wings are the largest and most effective surfaces of a flying insect and it is on them that the various forces interact. The most consistent force affecting an insect in flight is the force of gravity acting on its body and tending to cause it to fall. This force we call the weight of the insect and it acts vertically downwards. As the insect moves forwards in flight, air in its path is pushed aside. The air resists that movement and the force of

resistance is known as drag, a force which acts to prevent forward movement of the insect. These two forces – weight and drag – acting at right angles to each other, must be overcome if the insect is to fly.

You can experience for yourself a force equivalent to the drag on an insect wing. When driving at, say, sixty miles per hour on the motorway, place your hand flat and palm downwards, a little way out of the window. The air rushing past pushes against the leading edge of your hand, tending to force it backwards. If you now rotate your hand, tipping the leading edge upwards, the wind catches it increasingly underneath and an upward force is experienced in addition to the backward one. This upward component is known as lift and it varies with the angle at which your hand meets the wind. Technically, this is known as the angle of attack. The lift also varies, of course, with the strength of the wind experienced by your hand. This air movement, relative to your hand, is called the relative wind.

The same forces are experienced by the wing of a gliding insect. In still air, an insect gradually loses height as it glides forwards. Its progress, and the forces acting upon it, can be represented by a diagram. It achieves its relative wind by its forward motion, so the direction of the wind is opposite to that of the glide path. The weight of the insect (W) acts vertically downwards and may be represented

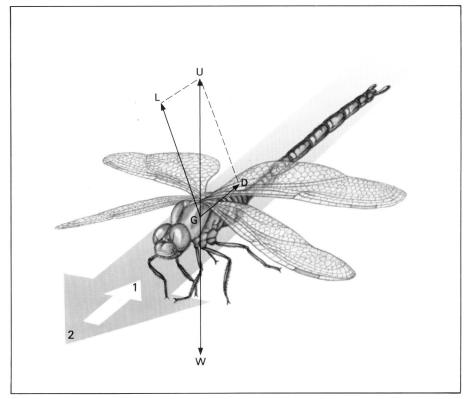

Diagram of the forces acting on a gliding insect. (1) Direction of relative wind, (2) glide path, (W) weight of insect, (G) centre of gravity, (D) drag, (L) lift, (U) resultant upward force. These forces and their interactions and significance are explained in the text.

on our diagram by a line whose length is proportional to the size of the force. Similarly, the drag (D) can be represented by a line drawn along the direction of the relative wind and the lift (L) by a line at right angles to that. Lift and drag are the two components of the resultant force produced by the action of the relative wind on the wing and their magnitudes are such that, when represented diagramatically, they compose a parallelogram of forces whose diagonal represents the resultant upward force (U), equal in magnitude and opposite in direction to the weight of the insect. In practice, the insect constantly adjusts the angle of attack of the two wings so that the resultant upward force is just a little less than the weight of the insect. This keeps the insect moving forwards and downwards in a shallow, controlled glide. It derives its power from the force of gravity and utilizes the resulting relative wind to derive lift.

If the air around the insect is actually moving, and especially if it is moving upwards, the insect no longer depends on the effect of the descent to produce all of the relative wind and in these circumstances it can obtain enough lift from the relative wind to remain at the same height or even to rise in the airstream.

This sort of consideration of angle of attack and of resultants of lift and drag forces all sounds very technical and theoretical. Can we be certain that these considerations are actually relevant to a gliding insect? It would, of course, be very difficult to measure such forces on a freely gliding insect but it is possible in a wind tunnel to produce a turbulence-free air stream of controlled speed to represent the relative wind. You can then mount a dead insect with outstretched wings on two very sensitive balances at right angles to each other to measure lift and drag. The whole apparatus can be rotated by controlled amounts in the airstream to compare the effects of different angles of attack. When the angle of attack is negative, the measured lift is also negative – the wind is pushing the insect downwards. As the angle is increased above 0° the lift increases till about 30° after which it may fall off quite rapidly. Flight with an angle of attack greater than 30° can be quite dangerous, especially near the ground, as the lift may suddenly deteriorate and cause a crash. This is the phenomenon which in aircraft is known as stalling. In fact, the deterioration of lift beyond the critical angle of attack is much less rapid in insects than in aircraft. Most aircraft stall readily with angles of attack above 20° but in the fruit-fly

Drosophila although lift decreases above 20° it does so only very slightly up to 60°, so that that particular insect is almost incapable of stalling.

As the angle of attack is increased from 0°, the drag also increases as a greater area of wing is presented to the wind. Since both lift and drag contribute to the resultant upward force it is useful to consider how these two forces together vary with angle of attack. Again this can be measured in our wind tunnel and it is found that all the aerodynamic forces are greatest at high angles of attack. These forces must be specially large at landing, when reduced forward speed decreases the relative wind. It is here again that insects have the advantage over aircraft because there is less likelihood that mistakes in orientation or sudden gusts of wind, producing excessive angles of attack, will result in catastrophic stalling.

Another interesting discovery made by the wind tunnel and balance apparatus is the importance of surface structures, such as hairs and scales, to the flight process. Lift and drag were measured at various angles of attack in a noctuid moth, then,

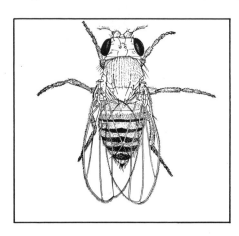

The fruit fly *Drosophila*, favourite for genetical studies, also distinguishes itself in flight. Although able to fly only weakly, it is remarkably stable in the air and is almost incapable of stalling.

with the scales on the forward half of the upper surface of the wings carefully removed, the measurements were repeated. The results for drag were the same as before but the lift was much reduced. The reason for this surprising result is that the aerodynamic properties of the wing depend on the behaviour of the boundary layer – an extremely thin layer of air which is in direct contact with the surface of the wing. The behaviour of this layer depends on the physical nature of the wing surface.

A Hover fly photographed in flight, probably while executing a turning manoeuvre as one wing is apparently moving faster than the other. The complex wing twisting which occurs during the wing beat is seen here.

The Action of Moving Wings. In the previous section we considered how insects could fly by gliding. But five minutes walk in a garden on a sunny day will confirm that nearly always in flight, insects' wings are not spread out stiffly, but beat rapidly up and down. Common knowledge that, one might say, but I wonder how many people know exactly how the wings beat 'up and down'. Nor is it an easy matter to find out because the wings beat so fast that all we see is a confused blur. It takes a high-speed cine camera to slow down for our eyes the complex sequence of an individual wing stroke.

In practice, a fast-flying insect, like a hover fly, can be tethered by a wire attached by a tiny blob of wax to the tip of its abdomen, and suspended facing the outlet of a wind tunnel. When the wind is switched on, the insect will often fly quite well and a short sequence may be filmed at up to 8,000 pictures per second. For purposes of analysis of the wing-beat sequence it is important to know what the fly was trying to do – was it climbing, banking, or diving? – and for a basic investigation it is most useful to film the insect in level flight at constant speed. To achieve this, the fly is tethered to a flight balance which is pivoted in three planes so that the insect can move within limits from side to side, up and down and also backwards and forwards as it gains or loses ground against the air current from the wind tunnel. When all three pivots are in the zero position, the fly is maintaining level flight at a speed equal to the air

speed and, when this occurs, switches associated with the pivots set the camera in motion and the film shoots through at high speed with a deafening siren-like howl.

Analysis of such film indicates that the wing undergoes four distinct types of movement in every wing beat. Firstly there is the up and down motion whose plane of movement is oblique to the long axis of the body so that the wings move downwards and forwards and upwards and backwards. Secondly, superimposed on this, the wings are rotated about their bases in a regular way during each stroke. Thirdly, at least part of each wing is twisted by differing air pressures during different parts of each stroke and fourthly, except in hovering, the whole wing moves forwards through the air as the insect progresses. So, you see, it was not quite adequate to say that the wings beat 'up and down'.

The effect of all this movement in terms of aerodynamic forces can be calculated as for gliding wings. The major difference, apart from the increased complexity, is that the moving wings are themselves chiefly responsible for the production of the relative wind. In fact, the complex twisting and the unexpected pattern of the wing stroke are devices to ensure that the wing almost always attacks the relative wind in such a way as to derive a useful resultant force in terms of lift and forward thrust – even during the upstroke! Although the forces of lift and thrust vary considerably during a wing beat,

51

insects have never been seen to proceed jerkily and it is thought that the inertia of the insect's body smooths out the fluctuations.

The overall effect of these varying forces during a wing beat is that air, approaching the insect from ahead, is caught by the wings and thrown backwards and downwards. The corresponding reaction felt by the insect's body is a force directed upwards and forwards. This can be resolved into the components of lift (upwards) and thrust (forwards) which match the forces of weight and drag and so enable the insect to fly. If the insect wishes to climb, it alters the wing beat so that the emergent air stream is directed more downwards and less backwards. This reduces thrust but increases lift so that the insect soars upwards. To turn in flight, the insect alters the amplitude, and hence the power, of the wing beat on opposite sides of the body and it turns towards the side producing less power.

What Makes the Wings Move. Despite the complexity of movements executed by the wings, the mechanisms involved in producing those movements are, in principle, elegantly simple. Much depends on the nature of the articulation of the wing with the side of the thorax and, indeed, in the more advanced insects the flight muscles are not attached to the wings at all but achieve their effect by distorting the articulation.

The thorax of the wing-bearing segments is a fairly rigid but elastic box whose sides and base are solidly joined together but whose lid is too small for the box and would slip inside but for the membrane joining it to the top of the sides. It is on the top of the sides that the wings are pivoted and their inner ends are hinged to the lid of the thoracic box. Upward movement of the wings is caused by muscles which are attached at one end to the bottom of the thoracic box and at the other end to its lid. Contraction of these muscles on each side of the thorax pulls the lid down into the box and with it the inner end of the wing is forced down so that, due to the lever effect, the bulk of the wing shoots upwards. Muscles such as these are called indirect flight muscles because they are not connected directly to the wings. In dragonflies and some other less advanced insects, the down beat of the wings is produced by direct muscles stretching from the bottom of the box onto the wing base outside the point of pivoting on the side of the thoracic box. Again the lever effect causes the wing to move rapidly over a large distance with a very slight shortening of the muscle. With this system of muscles all four wings could probably act

The ways in which muscles create wing beats in insects such as the Dragonfly (A, B) and the House fly (C, D). (1) Side, (2) base, (3) lid of thorax, (4) wings, (5) indirect, upbeat muscle, (6) downbeat muscles direct in Dragonfly (B) and indirect in House fly (D). Darker colouration indicates the pairs of muscles which are contracting in each situation.

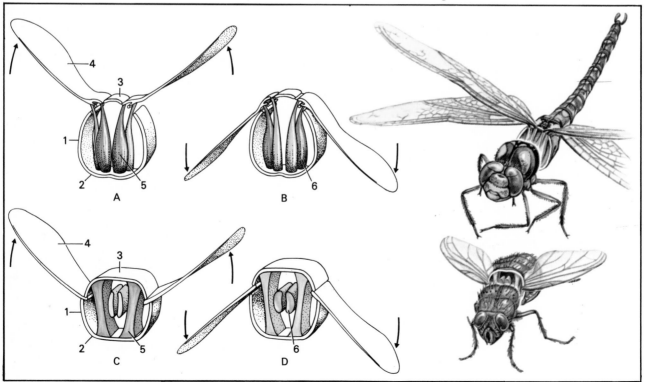

independently of each other, flapping up and down at different times and different rates. This, however, would not produce the forces necessary for controlled flight and, in practice, upbeat and downbeat movements are initiated for all four wings at the same time by synchronised nerve impulses from the central nervous system to the appropriate muscles.

This works very well for insects like the dragonfly whose wings beat at the relatively slow rate of 20 beats per second. If the nervous oscillator drifts a little and one wing falls slightly behind the other it is scarcely noticeable but in the flies and bees which have evolved wing beat frequencies up to 200 per second the problem is quite different. If one of the wings got out of phase there, the result would be disastrous but, in any case, the nervous system cannot produce impulses at such a high frequency. The problem is overcome in two ways.

Firstly the thoracic box is much stiffer, though still elastic, and the lid, much less flexible, moves as a single unit so that the wings on both sides of the body are obliged to do the same thing at the same time. The greater rigidity allows less movement so that, as the lid of the box is pulled down, the sides are pushed out like a tennis ball squashed top and bottom. Much of the energy in this deformation is stored in the elasticity of the thoracic box and is used to restore the original shape when the muscle pressure is released. To aid this conservation of energy, certain parts of the box and the wing-hinge mechanism are made of resilin – the most perfectly elastic substance ever produced by living organisms. In these more advanced insects, the down beat is not achieved by direct muscles attached to the wings but by another set of indirect muscles running from front to back of the thoracic box. Their contraction squashes the box in the opposite direction with the result that the lid pops up and forces the wing down.

The second modification for high frequency flight concerns the initiation of muscle contraction and again utilises the elasticity of the more rigid thoracic box. The wing joint mechanism is so constructed that it has two stable positions – with the wings either up or down – just like an electric light switch. When the wings move from one position to the other, they pass through a point of maximum instability – when the sides of the thoracic box are squashed outwards. As soon as the wings pass that point, the elasticity of the thorax flips them rapidly into the other stable position. This results in a sudden release of tension in the muscles which, in turn, induces them to contract again without having to wait for a nerve impulse. Hence the muscles can contract more rapidly than the nerves can fire, but the periodic nerve impulses are necessary to keep the system working. If you record the nerve impulses to the flight muscles of a fly in tethered flight, you discover that when it stops flying, and the nerve impulses cease, the wings beat for a further twelve cycles or so with declining amplitude before coming to rest.

The Control of Flight. The first feature of flight which requires control is the take-off. Many different stimuli will promote flight in an insect and the exact sequence of events at take-off varies. Often the legs catapult the insect into the air and loss of tarsal contact with the ground starts the flight motor. This works well in an insect where direct flight muscles under nervous control operate the wings, but in flies where the different flight muscles stimulate each other via the movements of the thorax produced by them, it needs something to start the cycle going. In other words, the main flight motor needs a starter motor to set it off. Typical of the economy of nature, the muscles which act as the starter motor also launch the fly into the air. On each

A Hover fly, master of helicopter flight, at rest on a flower. To analyse the complex and very rapid movements of its wings, the Hover fly can be tethered in flight and filmed at up to 8,000 pictures per second.

A Bee-hawk moth feeding on the wing from a flower. The fore legs steady the insect above the flower and the other two pairs are tucked up in the flight position. The proboscis is extended into the nectary and the insect maintains its position by rapid wing beats.

side of the thorax a muscle attached to the middle leg contracts powerfully, forcing the leg down and catapulting the fly into the air. At the same time, it gives a hefty downward tug to the lid of the thorax and the flight motor is started.

The speed of flight is carefully regulated by a complex computation, the details of which are unknown, involving an estimate of air speed measured by the antennae and an estimate of ground speed determined by the compound eyes. The speed of flight is governed by the power output of the flight

muscles and that, in turn, by the rate of nerve impulses from the central nervous system.

The control of flight direction is largely achieved by altering the orientation of the beating wings although, in some cases, the abdomen and legs may be used as rudders. In insects like the dragonfly, the activities of the direct flight muscles attached to individual wings can be varied independently to alter the direction of flight. The indirect flight muscles of the fly cannot affect the wings independently but the direct flight muscles have been retained and are used, not to produce power, but to alter the orientation of the wings and so direct the power output in different directions.

Apart from intentional deviations from a straight and level course, the insect may veer from its intended orientation because of gusts of wind or other hazards. It uses its sensory equipment, mainly the eyes and antennae, to monitor deviations in the three planes, pitch, roll and yaw, and can therefore initiate appropriate corrections. The most sophisticated flight control equipment is possessed by flies. Their halteres beat up and down in time with, but out of phase with, the wings. The relatively heavy knobbed ends of the halteres gives them an inertia which tends to keep them vibrating in the same plane all the time. The inertia is not sufficiently great to keep the insect in the same plane as well, but when the insect's flight deviates, the stalk of the haltere becomes twisted as the knob tries to maintain its original orientation. The stalk is richly supplied with sense organs called campaniform sensilla, or strain gauges which monitor the direction and extent of the deviation so that, if the fly did not intend it to happen, it can make the appropriate correction.

In addition to acting as a catapult on take-off, the legs must act as shock absorbers on landing. The approach of the ground detected by the eyes, acts as the stimulus for the extension of the legs from their folded position during flight. The legs grip the substratum with claws, spines and sticky pads. Unlike an aeroplane, the insect does not run forward after landing, so the legs have to perform a prodigious feat of braking. In landing on an unyielding tree trunk, a beetle such as the cockchafer strikes the trunk with outstretched legs at 6 ft 6 in (2 m) per second and in less than a quarter of an inch (6·5 mm) its body has come to rest. It has decelerated at about 1,225 ft (400 m) per second – and experienced a force of about 40g!

The means by which a fly can land upside down on a ceiling has long been a source of speculation. Does it have to fly upside down? Does it fly just below the ceiling and roll over at the last minute? Neither. Again the high-speed cine camera has shown us the answer. The fly approaches the ceiling at about 10 in (25 cm) per second, flying upwards at a steep angle. It then flies straight at the ceiling and stretches out all three pairs of legs. As its front feet touch and grip the ceiling it stops flying but its momentum carries it on and it pivots on its fore legs, belly up, and grips the ceiling with its other two pairs of legs to land with perfect control.

The predatory Robber fly shows the modification of each hind wing into a haltere, a stalk with a knob at the end. This organ, coloured white in this Robber fly, gives the insect information about its orientation in flight and enables it to control its flight path.

Food and Feeding

Since insects are an enormously numerous, diverse and widespread group, it is inevitable that their intake of food constitutes a very significant factor in the economy of nature. To take one example, in natural grassland insects convert plant material into their own body tissue more efficiently, and in at least as great a quantity, as do the mammalian herbivores. Since these insects may themselves be eaten, they form an essential link between green plants, the primary producers, and a wide range of other animals which are unable to utilize plant material directly.

What Insects Eat. The great diversity of insects is reflected in the very wide variety of plant and animal material, dead or alive, which constitutes their food. The more primitive insects living today, namely the Diplura, Thysanura, Protura and Collembola, exist largely on the dead and decaying remains of plants and especially on the fungi and bacteria causing that decay. They are consequently very important in the progressive breakdown of decaying organic material, a process vital to the continued fertility of the soil. It is suggested that ancestral insects, living in the moist litter of forest floors, had a similar diet. However, this so-called saprophytic diet is not restricted today to the primitive insects, as many of the more advanced types having soil-dwelling larvae, such as the beetles, still utilize these materials throughout their larval lives.

On the other hand, living plants today provide food for the majority of insects and the habits of many insects have evolved along with the plants. Although many feed on the roots or burrow in the stems or woody trunks of plants, most of the plant-eating, or phytophagous, insects eat leaves. The method of feeding on leaves varies; some stay on the outside and, like locusts and grasshoppers, bite off

fragments, or like aphids, pierce the leaf with tubular mouthparts through which they suck its fluid contents. Yet others penetrate and enter the leaves, feeding within them but leaving the outer layers intact, so that mines and galleries are formed within the leaves. Such leaf-miners include the larvae of some butterflies, moths, flies, bees and wasps.

With the evolution of flowering plants a whole new range of associations developed, as adult butterflies, moths, flies, bees, wasps and beetles took to feeding on flowers, and evolved modifications for obtaining nectar and pollen while at the same time fertilizing the flowers. At the same period, in the Mesozoic, the larvae of these flower-frequenting flies

Left: The head of a Stag beetle larva showing the powerful jaws. The general body cuticle of this soil-dwelling larva is soft but the large mandibles are hardened and darkened, especially at the tips and at their joints with the head capsule.

Right: Sawfly larvae on a sallow bush. This picture dramatically illustrates the effect which caterpillars can have on vegetation. This devastation can be repeated over a whole plant or, in crop species, over many acres of plants resulting in enormous losses of food for man.

and beetles were learning to obtain their food in the warm fermenting faeces and decaying bodies of the warm-blooded vertebrates which were becoming the dominant large fauna. Some flies and bugs developed the ability to pierce the skin of mammals and feed on blood, thus becoming parasites. Yet others became specialized as predators, killing and devouring smaller insects and other animals.

A few insects, such as the cockroach, are more or less omnivorous but most have some degree of specificity and in a few cases the specificity may be absolute – the diet being restricted to one species of host plant or animal. Amongst the bugs (Homoptera) *Coccus fagi* only feeds on beech and the larvae of the sawfly *Xyela julii* only on the pine tree *Pinus sylvestris*. Some insects which normally show great specificity can feed on other plants if forced to do so, but others will die in the absence of their preferred plant. At the other end of the range, even insects like the Desert locust, which will eat a wide variety of plants, do usually show some preferences. Amongst predaceous insects, the wasp *Philanthus* only catches bees, and pompilid wasps only take certain species of spiders, but the robber flies (asilids) take any flying insects of suitable size, including members of their own species. The free-living blood-sucking insects, such as the mosquitoes, bite a wide range of mammalian and bird hosts but the less mobile blood-suckers are, of necessity, more specific. Thus lice, which pass their whole life history on the body of the host, are extremely specific. The young of fleas develop in the nests of their hosts and tend to be restricted to nests which occur in particular micro-habitats – underground or in trees, for example. This, of course, limits the type of host normally encountered but most fleas will bite unusual hosts, given the chance.

Finding and Recognizing Food. Food finding plays an important part in the lives of most insects. Exceptions are those which find themselves surrounded by food from the moment of hatching, but that usually occurs because the female parent has done the food finding for them by laying her eggs on a suitable host plant or animal. Similarly, the larvae of social insects are fed by the workers, but generally each individual must fend for itself.

Phytophagous insects, that is, those that feed on plants, may recognize the presence of potential food at a distance by its appearance. They may be attracted towards an object of appropriate size and colour, particularly if it shows a pattern of vertical stripes. Aphids are attracted to yellow which may be related to the fact that they prefer young or senescent leaves, which are usually more yellow than mature ones. Smell can also be a useful guide to insects seeking plants from a distance. Bees, having made a visual approach to a flower, are guided by the smell of the flower and by their own colony smell previously left on the flower. Larvae of the desert locust which have been deprived of food will respond to the odour of crushed grass by moving upwind. The odour is perceived by the numerous sense organs called olfactory sensilla on the antennae and such a response would lead them to the food plant. Often, however, leaf-eating insects do not have to locate their food from a distance, because between meals they remain resting on the food plant.

At close quarters, taste receptors are used. These so-called chemoreceptors may be present on the feet as well as on the mouth-parts. Quite often insects assess the palatability of a plant by testing it with a series of receptors on different parts of the body and only if the plant passes the test of acceptability at each successive level will it eventually be eaten. A locust, attracted to a plant by its smell, will test it with the chemoreceptors on its feet as it walks over the plant surface. If the result is favourable it will then vibrate its maxillary and labial palps so that the hundreds of taste sensilla on the palp tips are brought into numerous brief contacts with the leaf surface. These sensilla are apparently sensitive to materials in the cuticle of the plant leaf and the locust can distinguish between, for example, a palatable grass leaf and a non-palatable daisy leaf on the basis of this test alone. If the palp test gives a favourable result, the locust then lowers its head so that the labrum, or upper lip, touches the leaf surface and the animal moves over the surface till an edge is found from which it takes an exploratory bite. This releases fluids from within the leaf which are in turn tested by sensilla inside the mouth cavity. Only if the plant passes this final test will continuous feeding start.

It is of considerable interest to know just what is being tasted in these elaborate test procedures and much recent research has been designed to find this out. It appears that nutritionally valuable substances, like sugars, present in plants will promote feeding. However, most plants contain adequate nutrients to satisfy the needs of most insects so that selection between plants cannot be made on the basis of palatable nutrient materials alone. Probably some nutritional substances are inhibitory to some insects, depending on their concentration in the plant, so that the balance of stimulatory and inhibitory substances will make a plant acceptable to some insects and not to others.

Additionally there is a wide range of non-nutritional substances which can similarly promote acceptance or rejection of plants possessing them. Often these substances have no known nutritional value for the plant and it is thought that they have evolved in plants as a means of defence against insects. Thus the Cruciferae, the family containing the various species of cabbage, characteristically contain quite high concentrations of mustard oils which repel many insects. But evolution is a process of constant change and some insects have become tolerant of these inhibitory substances, and even in some cases have come to require them as essential stimulants for the plant to be acceptable as food. Thus the larvae of the cabbage white butterfly *Pieris* normally eat only plants containing mustard oils.

An extreme example of an inhibitory substance is azadirachtin which occurs in the Indian neem tree *Azadirachta indica*. The substance occurs in all parts of the tree and gives it protection against a wide range of insects. An extract from the seeds of the neem tree has been used to spray on other plants and is found to give them some protection against insect attack.

The problem of food finding is rather different for predators. The sense chiefly used, at least in effecting the initial capture, is vision since it alone can give a sufficiently rapid and directed response to moving prey. The wasp *Philanthus* reacts to any moving insect of appropriate size but only catches bees – or insects which have artificially been made to smell of bees. Thus the closer inspection involves the olfactory sense. *Philanthus* only strings a captured insect if it actually is a bee, and any other insect, to which the experimenter has applied 'bee odour', is released. It is thought that this final recognition is tactile.

Similar behaviour has been found in other predators, but an alternative to the active pursuit is to sit still and wait for the prey to come within range. This is the tactic employed by the Praying mantis and the mechanism by which it catches its prey is described later. A similar waiting game is played by ant lions, the larvae of some Neuroptera. The larva digs a funnel-shaped pit in dry sand and lies buried at the bottom with only its head, and formidable jaws, exposed. When an ant walks over the edge, it slithers down to the bottom as the sandy slopes of the pit slip away from under its feet. The larva ensures the ant's downfall by flicking sand at it as it struggles to regain the top. When the ant slips to the bottom of the pit its fate is sealed.

Blood-sucking parasites use similar sequences of visual, chemical and mechanical stimuli to find and recognize their hosts. Similarly, with internal parasites, the adult female usually selects a suitable host. Sometimes, however, the larvae have to find the host for themselves. The Human warble fly *Cordylobia anthropophaga* lays her eggs in sand fouled by urine, and the larvae, which hatch in a day or two, remain

A honeybee collecting pollen from apple blossom. The body is covered with branched hairs which trap the sticky pollen. Later the bee combs the pollen into the special 'pollen baskets', seen here on the hind legs, before transporting it back to the hive. Bees also use their long tongues to obtain nectar from flowers.

The head of a Giant cricket. The finger-like processes hanging from the underside of the head are sensory palps. Sense organs on the tips of these palps are used to test potential food. The upper lip conceals the powerful jaws behind.

inactive until a suitable host comes near. They are then activated by the vibrations and warmth of the host and bore through the skin.

How Insects Feed on Plants. Having selected a plant, the insect's next problem is that of holding the food and getting it into the mouth. The principal cutlery used by the insect, apart from its feet, are its mouthparts and just as there is an enormous variety of food material, so the apparently different types of mouthparts are very numerous. But it will be no surprise to the student of biology to learn that the apparent variety of mouthparts merely represent numerous modifications of the same basic plan.

The basic arrangement is found in insects which chew their food, whatever its nature, and was evolved by the early omnivorous and plant-eating species and has remained substantially unchanged for millions of years. These chewing mouthparts occur today in the adults and larvae of at least fifteen orders and are well seen in grasshoppers and cockroaches. The upper lip, or labrum, is a flap-like extension hanging down from the front of the face. Behind this is a pair of powerful jaws, or mandibles, which close in from the sides like secateurs. Between the bases of the mandibles lies a relatively small opening, the mouth proper. Behind the mouth, in the midline, is the tongue-like hypopharynx behind which the salivary duct opens. On either side of the hypopharynx is another, less powerful pair of jaws, the maxillae. They are used for holding the food and feeding it between the mandibles to be crushed and sheared. In addition to their pincer-like points, the maxillae each have a fleshy lobe, the galea, which act as lateral lips to the mouth cavity, and also a finger-like palp bearing many sense organs. The lower lip of the mouth cavity is formed by the labium, a structure derived in the course of evolution from a second pair of maxillae, but today fused in the midline to form a single fleshy lobe bearing another pair of sensory palps.

Where this basic plan has been altered in the course of evolution, it is by the addition of new structures or the modification of old structures to

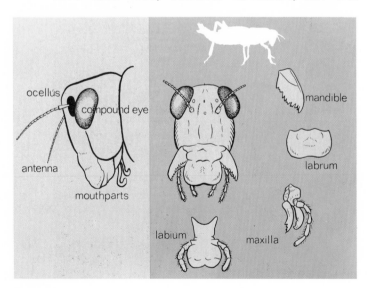

Diagram of the head of a locust showing the mouthparts in position and separated out on the right. The labrum and labium are single structures forming the upper and lower lips. The paired mandibles and maxillae are jaws which move laterally.

60

perform a new function. Mosquito larvae feed on the very fine particles, algae and bacteria, suspended in the pond water in which they live. Mandibles and maxillae alone cannot cope with such fine food but are still present. Additionally there are, on the front of the head, tufts of long hairs which set up currents as the insect sweeps them to and fro through the water. These currents, directed towards the mouth, pass through rows of closely set bristles on the mandibles and maxillae on which the food particles are caught, formed into a mass and then swallowed.

A new structure has been formed from existing parts in the honey bees. Unlike the sharp pincer-like mandibles of the predatory wasps and ants, those of the bee are flat and blunt and are used to mould the wax for the honey-comb. But to reach the nectar deep in the centres of flowers, a long tongue is necessary. It is formed by a long, flexible, strap-like extension of the labium. The sides of the tongue are curved down and inwards, almost meeting below to form a tube which is enclosed by the equally long, strap-like labial and maxillary palps. The tip of the tongue protrudes beyond the end of the tube and its much grooved and hairy surface causes food to stick to it before being sucked into the tube.

A similar function is fulfilled by the coiled tongue of a butterfly but this is formed in a totally different

A butterfly (left) with tongue coiled but visible in front of the head. An enlarged frontal view of the head (centre) with the tongue uncoiling. A section of the tongue (right) showing how the two parts come together to form a tube down the centre.

way. The grooved inner surfaces of the enormously elongated galeae are held together by interlocking bristles along their lengths acting like zip fasteners, the two grooves coming together to form the sucking tube. In the relaxed state, an elastic rod in the dorsal surface of the proboscis keeps it coiled up. When a

The mouthparts of the Black bean aphid. The very slender, needle-like mandibles and maxillae are seen protruding from the tip of the sheath formed by the almost tubular labrum. The mandibles lie together to form a double tube for the passage of saliva into and juices out of the plant cells pierced by the aphid.

butterfly wishes to extend it, muscles along its length bend the upper surface round so that the proboscis straightens out like a steel measuring tape. Most butterflies drink nectar or juices on the surface of plants but the tropical noctuid moth *Anomis* has spines at the tip of the proboscis with which it lacerates fruit, causing much damage in orchards.

A different type of modification enables the fragile aphid to pierce the tough cuticle and outer layers of plants and probe its way into the vessels or veins

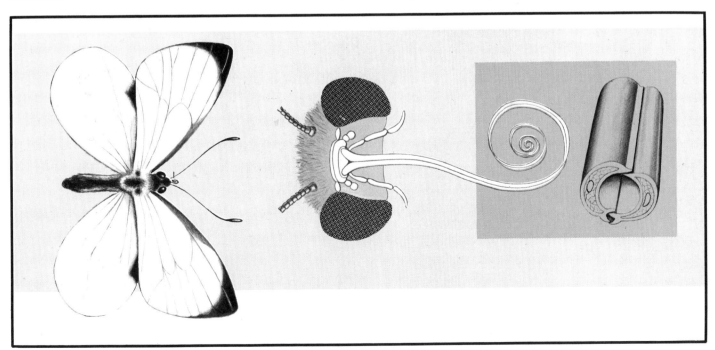

The Praying mantis *Mantis religiosa*, about to make a meal of a spider. This insect, common in southern Europe and North Africa, gets its name from the habit of sitting motionless with the fore legs raised and held together as if it were praying.

How Insects Feed on Animals. Even insects well equipped with chewing mandibles normally only imbibe the juices of their victims and many are adapted to suck juices only. Thus many bugs (Heteroptera) which are predatory or parasitic on other insects or vertebrates have mouthparts essentially similar in form and function to those of the plant-feeding aphids. Other methods of forming sucking tubes by the apposition of grooved mouthparts are common. When the hapless ant has fallen to the bottom of the ant lion's pit, it is impaled on either side by huge, curved mandibles and maxillae. The body fluids are sucked up through channels formed between each mandible and maxilla. Similarly, in the larvae of the giant diving beetle *Dytiscus*, each mandible has an almost closed groove on its inner surface which acts as a sucking tube. This of course is a useful technique for obtaining body fluids under water. A less sophisticated but equally remarkable method is used by the aquatic larvae of dragonflies. They lie concealed in mud at the bottom of the pond then, judging the distance perfectly, they seize their prey with a sudden

Right: The Purple emperor butterfly *Apatura iris* using its tubular proboscis to suck up sweet fluids from the surface of a plant. The long proboscis can also be extended deep into flowers to obtain nectar. Commonly in butterflies, the fore legs are reduced and are not used in walking.

Below: The Mantisfly *Mantispa interrupta* seizing a fly in its spiked front legs. After waiting motionless until the unsuspecting prey come within reach, the mantis shoots out its front legs to grasp the other insect and bring it within range of its mandibles.

from which it feeds. The proboscis which you see held beneath the head of the aphid is the almost tubular labium which merely acts as a sheath for the incredibly slender, needle-like mandibles and maxillae within. Each mandible bears two longitudinal grooves on its inner surface and, as the mandibles lie together, these grooves form two tubes, one through which saliva is pumped to lubricate the passage of the stylets into the plant, and the other through which food is pumped out. The maxillary stylets are barbed at their tips which helps to anchor the mouthparts in the plant.

movement of the labium. In this case, the labium is greatly elongated and can be held folded under the head when not in use or extended by suddenly increasing the blood pressure in the organ. The palps have been modified to form two formidable hooks on which the prey is impaled and drawn back to the mandibles by the retraction of the labium.

Thus one commonly finds that in different insects, the same job is done by different structures. In part this reflects what is known to biologists as Dollo's Law: if a structure is lost in the course of evolution and the animal later develops a need for it, the original structure is never regained but a different one is modified to fulfil the original function. This is well illustrated in the evolution of mouthparts of the Diptera. The piercing equipment of the mosquito is similar to that of aphids; the piercing mandibles and maxillae play a prominent role and the labium is a soft sheath. The horse-flies, or tabanids, inflict an equally troublesome bite using serrated mandibles which cut the skin like scissors and pointed maxillae which stab vigorously. The blood which this assault releases is taken up in a tube formed from the labrum and hypopharynx which is plunged into the wound. Additionally, the softer labium ends in two fleshy lobes with grooves on the underside which converge at the base of the sucking tube. In an alternative mode of feeding, this grooved pad or labellum is spread on the bleeding surface and fluid gathered up by the converging grooves.

Various of the more advanced flies, like the blow-flies and the housefly *Musca* have developed the labellum mode of feeding. They have lost all the piercing mouthparts and imbibe juices found on the surface of plants or animals. But some tropical species of *Musca* have developed a taste for blood and harass other biting flies away so that they may feed from the wounds which they themselves are incapable of inflicting. Some species, however, have tooth-like projections on the labellum with which they scratch the surface of drying wounds and others have these well enough developed to pierce the skin for themselves. The most effective development of this modification occurs in the tsetse fly *Glossina* in which the long slender labium is microscopically toothed at the tip and protected in a sheath formed by the maxillary palps. The toothed tip of the labellum is invaginated like the tip of a glove finger. As this invagination is rapidly pushed out and in, the teeth lining it cut effortlessly through the skin with a delicacy which often leaves the victim unaware of the attack.

The Gut and Digestion. The gut of insects is, like that of most animals, a more or less simple tube

A female scorpionfly *Panorpa communis* feeding on the pupa of a Small tortoiseshell butterfly. The head is drawn out downwards into a snout or rostrum which carries the biting mouthparts.

running through the inside of the body from mouth to anus. By doubling back or coiling within the insect, the gut can be appreciably longer than the insect itself. In general, the food passes slowly but steadily backwards through the gut whilst being

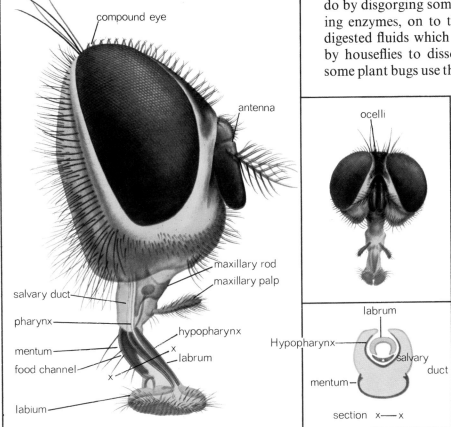

salvary duct
pharynx
mentum
food channel
labium
compound eye
antenna
maxillary rod
maxillary palp
hypopharynx
x
labrum
x

ocelli

labrum
Hypopharynx
mentum
salvary
duct
section x—x

The mouthparts of the fly. Left: head in side view with mouthparts in section to show the complex tube, shown also in the cross-section bottom right, through which liquid food is sucked up through the tongue (labellum) into the mouth. Top right: mouthparts in front view.

cuticular lining of part of the foregut has been formed into teeth. Contractions of the muscular gut wall around this region cause the teeth to grind the food like a mill.

Many insects which cannot grind their food in this way, digest it outside of the body instead. This they do by disgorging some of the gut contents, containing enzymes, on to the food, then sucking up the digested fluids which result. This technique is used by houseflies to dissolve their potential food and some plant bugs use the proboscis to inject into plant

attacked by digestive enzymes. These chemicals promote the breakdown of carbohydrates, fats and proteins in the food into simpler, smaller molecules which may be more readily absorbed through the gut wall into the blood. The insect gut is divided anatomically and functionally into three regions, the foregut, the midgut and the hindgut.

The foregut is an invagination of the outer body layer, the epidermis, and as such is lined with cuticle. This cuticle prevents the secretion of enzymes from the cells into the lumen or the absorption of food in the reverse direction. Consequently, the foregut is often used for the initial storage of food from a meal, either liquid or solid, and may be much enlarged for this purpose. Some digestion does occur in this region due to enzymes added to the food with the saliva or regurgitated into the foregut from the midgut behind. In some insects, like grasshoppers and cockroaches, which take in coarse food, the

cells enzymes which dissolve the stored starch grains. The same method is used by many predaceous beetles. Those grooved mandibles of the aquatic larvae of *Dytiscus* are used to inject the stomach contents into the impaled prey. The powerful digestive juices render the internal organs of the victim into a soup within minutes and this is then sucked up through the grooves in the mandibles.

The midgut, in which most of the digestion and absorption occurs, does not have a cuticular lining. To protect the fragile cells from hard materials in the food, the gut wall is lined by a delicate but tough network of chitin fibres. Seen at the great magnification of the electron microscope, this 'peritrophic membrane' looks like a fine net curtain and through the pores the enzymes and digested food pass to and from the midgut cells. The midgut is usually a simple tube but may have modifications associated with certain diets. Plant fluids are very

65

dilute and contain little nourishment. This is not a problem for flies, butterflies, or bees which take these fluids only as adults when most of their growth is complete, but the Homoptera and some Heteroptera rely on plant fluids for their entire growth. They must therefore take in very large quantities of fluid and, in order to avoid diluting the blood excessively, the surplus water must be eliminated rapidly. In cicads, the anterior midgut forms a large, thin-walled bladder which is closely bound to the hindgut into which water passes directly, leaving the nutritious fluid sufficiently concentrated for the enzymes to act effectively on it.

The hindgut is lined with a cuticle which is much thinner and more permeable than that of the foregut. The chief function of this region is the resorption of water and other materials from the urine but occasionally other unusual functions are fulfilled. In wood-eating termites, a large expansion of the hindgut houses vast numbers of protozoan flagellates which may account for a third of the weight of the insect. These flagellates are capable of digesting the cellulose of which the wood is largely composed, whereas the termites themselves cannot digest this material. In this symbiotic or co-operative relationship the flagellates are provided with a home and a supply of food and the insect lives on the break-down products of the cellulose provided by the flagellates.

The Need for Food. Food is needed for two major activities: to provide material for growth and reproduction, and to provide material for respiration and energy production. The energy for muscular and other bodily activities is mainly provided by sugar

A weevil or snout beetle. These beetles are characterized by a long drawn out head which terminates in a snout or rostrum seen clearly in this picture. The mouthparts are situated at the tip of this snout and the mandibles are powerful and capable of chewing hard vegetable matter such as seeds and wood. That this specialized feeding mechanism is successful is evidenced by the fact that weevils form the largest family in the Animal Kingdom with over 35,000 species.

Food and Feeding

and this has already been discussed. The requirements for growth are more demanding and involve complex mixtures of carbohydrates, fats, proteins, salts, vitamins and water just as in all other animals. Although most of these requirements must be present in the diet of growing or reproducing insects at all times, some may be obtained from other sources.

Sometimes an otherwise essential nutrient is not required in the diet because sufficient reserves of it have been accumulated at an earlier period. Such a reserve occurs in the yolk of insect eggs. Since the yolk is very small, it does not store major nutrients like glucose, but sufficient vitamins may be present to see the insect through the larval life. Large stores of nutrients may be built up in the fat body during larval life so that in some cases, as in some Lepidop-

tera, the adults do not need to feed at all.

Most insects living on a good mixed diet have no problems with dietary requirements but those living on restricted diets have had to overcome such problems, often in remarkable ways. Mammalian blood is extremely nutritious but is deficient in some vitamins, especially of the B group. All those insects which eat only blood throughout their entire life, the tsete fly *Glossina*, the sucking lice Anoplura, the bugs *Cimex* and *Rhodnius*, for example, all contain micro-organisms living in specialized cells called mycetocytes. These cells are usually in parts of the gut. The micro-organisms, yeasts or bacteria, synthesize the missing nutrients and make them available to the insect. These essential micro-organisms are transferred from parent to offspring, often by invading the eggs before they are laid.

A Tiger beetle *Magacephala denticollis* of Nigeria devouring a grasshopper. The popular name for this group of beetles is well deserved as they are formidable predators with large, sharply toothed jaws, perhaps the most ferocious and voracious of insects.

One of the characteristics of our planet is that it receives radiant energy from outer space, mainly from the sun. The waves of that radiation constitute a broad band of varying wavelengths called the electromagnetic spectrum. Only a small part of the spectrum can be detected by living organisms, and part of that is what we ourselves recognize as light, the different wavelengths giving us the sensations which we call the colours of the spectrum.

To investigate whether a given insect can see and if so, how, and in what way its visual capabilities relate to our own, we need to know something of the mechanism of vision. The basic requirement for detecting radiant energy is the possession of a chemical or chemicals capable of absorbing the energy. Such chemicals are common in nature and usually absorb some wavelengths of the spectrum maximally whilst reflecting others. When white light, such as that from the sun, containing all the spectral colours mixed together, falls on a chemical of this sort, the chemical appears coloured because we see the light it reflects, which produces the colour associated with the wavelengths remaining unabsorbed. Thus a red pigment absorbs all except the red wavelengths, a white pigment absorbs hardly any of the light and a black pigment absorbs almost all of it.

The absorption of light by a chemical may cause an electrochemical reaction to occur in it, such as those made use of in photography. If light-sensitive chemicals of this kind were incorporated into cells in such a way that the products or effects of the reaction could stimulate the nervous system, then we would have the second element required for the mechanism of vision, and in such a light-sensitive, cellular, system we would have the rudiments of an organ of vision. Such an organ would be capable of distinguishing light from dark and registering changes in light intensity, but would give its owner no information about the intricacies of structural form and texture which are almost always present in our surroundings.

One of the reasons for the great success of insects is their acute vision, especially in carnivorous species. In this ichneumon fly, the large compound eyes are clearly visible as are the three dorsal ocelli situated on top of the head.

To achieve this, it is necessary to condense the wide visual field around us to fit within the narrow confines of a visual organ. This, of course, is what a lens does when it produces a small image of the visual field and projects it onto a surface within the visual organ. In addition to a lens system, the visual organ must have its individual light-sensitive cells sufficiently small and sufficiently numerous to distinguish between, and react differently to, different parts of the image. And finally, to achieve cognition of the visual field, the animal must have a nervous system of sufficient organizational complexity and functional sophistication to register and act upon the visual information which its receptor organs are capable of providing. We shall see that, in the insects, these different levels of organization of visual organs have given rise to four types of visual capability mediated by the dermal light sense, dorsal ocelli, stemmata and, most important of all, the compound eyes.

The Dermal Light Sense. The simplest and perhaps the most mysterious light sensitivity occurring in insects is the dermal light sense. In insects having this sense, there appear to be receptors in the general surface of the body, but no specific sense organs mediating this response have ever been located. A number of insects with normal visual organs, including some cockroaches and lepidopterous larvae, still respond to light when all their known visual receptors are covered. Some cockroaches will avoid the light even when decapitated! A similar light-avoidance response occurs in some blind, cave-dwelling insects such as the beetle *Anophthalmus*. Sometimes, in addition to a general light-sensitivity all over the body, a particular region may have enhanced sensitivity. Thus in the larvae of the aquatic beetle *Dytiscus*, there is maximum sensitivity around the spiracles at the tip of the abdomen. When the larva comes to the surface to breathe, it is this area which makes contact with the surface of the water and is therefore best placed to monitor changes in light intensity which might herald the approach of a predator. Changes of less immediate significance are detected by light-sensitive cells in the brain of some aphids. In this case, day length is the factor detected and, depending on whether it is longer or shorter than 14 hours, it causes, as we shall see later, reproduction to be either parthenogenetic or sexual.

Except in the last example, where the sensitive cells are in the brain itself, the connection between the receptor cells and the nervous system is not clear. However, the larvae of Cyclorrhapha (eg houseflies and blowflies) have a group of innervated, light-sensitive cells deep within the tissues at the head end. These cells mediate a characteristic response of the larva which is known as negative phototaxis. A taxis is an orientated movement made in response to some stimulus, such as light. The phototaxis of the larva is said to be negative because the animal moves away from the source of stimulation. It moves in a direct line away from light by turning so that the light-sensitive cells are shaded by the rest of the body. It is

The Cuckoo wasp (right), and the Queen wasp *Polistes* (below) show clearly the occurrence of dorsal ocelli. There are three of these small visual organs forming a triangle on top of the head between the two, much larger, compound eyes. Each ocellus has a number of sensory cells under the cuticle which respond to light but these organs probably do not report visual images to the brain. Instead, these organs are very sensitive to changes in light intensity and appear to regulate the state of alertness of the insect.

thought that these strange organs are a degenerate form of the more elaborate stemmata.

Dorsal Ocelli. Many adult insects and larvae of hemimetabolous insects have, in addition to compound eyes, small visual organs called dorsal ocelli. There are typically three of these, forming a small triangle on top of the head.

The cuticle above each organ is transparent and may either be quite flat or biconvex, thus acting as a lens. Beneath the lens, the epidermal cells are also transparent, allowing light to pass to the nerve cells of the retina lying immediately below. There is usually a large number of nerve cells grouped together in units of two, three or four. Distally, each cell of a unit contributes to a central, specialized, region containing visual pigment and in which light energy can stimulate the nerve cell. In this region, the inner surface of each cell of a unit is produced into fingerlike projections which are thought to contain the visual pigment. This specialized area of each cell is called a rhabdomere and the rhabdomeres of the several cells in each unit are known as the rhabdom. Usually pigment cells surround the whole organ and sometimes individual units within the organ are screened from each other by pigment-containing cells. Alternatively, as in the cockroach, there is no pigment at all and the eye is surrounded by a reflecting layer. This is formed by cells which probably contain whitish urate crystals and has the effect of throwing light back into the eye, thus affording a second opportunity of its being absorbed.

Where there is a cuticular lens, a fairly sharp image is formed but it appears that this has little or no significance since the image falls some distance behind the retina. Thus the ocelli cannot be used for form vision. They are, however, very sensitive to low light intensities and to small changes in light intensity. This is enhanced by the fact that the axons from the large number of nerve cells converge onto a much smaller number of second order cells conveying the stimulation to the brain. In the dragonfly *Sympetrum* there are about 675 nerve cells but in the ocellar nerve leading to the brain there is one large axon, two medium sized axons and a few smaller ones.

The use which insects make of the ocelli is not very clear but they seem to be concerned somehow in regulating light-directed behaviour. The cockroach *Periplaneta* exhibits a diurnal rhythm of activity in which it is most active in the dark. This rhythm is not maintained if the ocelli are covered over. The fruit-fly *Drosophila* is more alert to changes in light intensity perceived by the compound eyes when the ocelli are intact. Thus the ocelli are considered to be stimulatory organs enhancing the responses of the nervous system to external stimuli.

Stemmata. Whilst dorsal ocelli occur along with compound eyes in the hemimetabolous larvae, the only visual organs of holometabolous larvae are stemmata, sometimes called lateral ocelli. They vary in form from mere pigmented spots equipped with refractive bodies, to the complex organs of the larval tiger beetle *Cicindela*. That larva bears, on each side of the head, six stemmata, two of which have more than 6,000 nerve cells each. Tenthredinid larvae (Hymenoptera) have, on each side of the head, one stemma which is very like a dorsal ocellus in structure, having a cuticular lens and numerous nerve cells arranged in groups. However, the most thoroughly studied stemmata are those of lepidopterous larvae and these are rather different. There are six on each side of the head and each one has two lenses. There is a cuticular lens as before and underneath it a tiny crystalline lens secreted by three cells. This lens forms more or less distinct, inverted images. Associated with this double lens system, there are, in the caterpillar *Isia isabella*, seven heavily pigmented receptor cells, three meeting in the midline to form a rhabdom distally, while the other four form a more

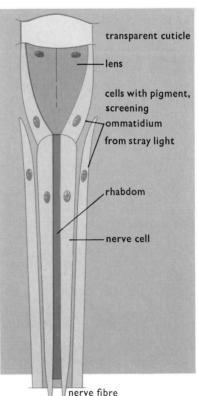

transparent cuticle

lens

cells with pigment, screening ommatidium from stray light

rhabdom

nerve cell

Detail of a single ommatidium, thousands of which form the compound eye. Only the transparent cuticle, which acts as an additional lens, is seen from the surface. Light energy is thought to be detected in the rhabdom which is part of the nerve cells. The nerve fibres convey the resulting electrical stimulation to the brain.

nerve fibre

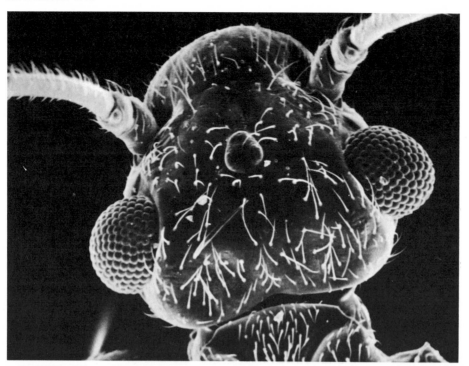

Left: A photograph taken with the stereoscan electron microscope of the head of a psocid *Graphopsocus cruciatus*. The large, bulbous compound eyes are prominent on either side of the head. The many facets seen on the surface of each eye are the cuticular lenses of individual ommatidia.

Right: The head of a Horse fly showing the remarkable colour patterns typical of the compound eyes of this family (Tabanidae). This irridescence is due to the form of the ommatidia and disappears on death.

Below: A grasshopper sitting in an alert posture on the surface of a leaf. Notice the large compound eyes high on each side of the head, well placed to monitor the surrounding environment and give early warning of any danger. One of the dorsal ocelli is situated between the compound eye and the base of the antenna.

proximal rhabdom. As with a fixed-focus camera, the image falls somewhere along the length of the rhabdom regardless of the distance of the object from the stemma. However, because of the small number of cells in the rhabdom, image reception cannot be very efficient and it seems likely that the main function of the lens is in concentrating the light. Vision in this insect is the sum of the visual capacities of all the stemmata working together. Each stemma registers light intensity from that part of the visual field at which it is pointed. Since the fields of the stemmata do not overlap, the insect will see a very coarse mosaic of 12 points of light, six from each side of the head. Yet a caterpillar can differentiate shapes, recognize vertical pillars and orientate to black-white boundaries – all this even when 11 of the 12 stemmata have been blacked over. It is able to do this because it improves on its coarse mosaic by moving the head from side to side whilst crawling. Thus it scans a wider visual field and, like a human feeling an object in the dark, it explores the

contours of dark objects and is able to estimate their approximate shape. Even in the tiger beetle larvae, whose stemmata have large numbers of retinal elements, it is believed that all the stemmata function together as a unit. These larvae live in short vertical burrows in sandy soil where they lie with heads out waiting for prey to pass within range of their mandibles. The stemmata enable the larva to judge this range accurately and also to estimate the size of the prey. If it is larger than 0·12–0·16 in (3–4 mm), the larva will withdraw into its burrow rather than attack.

Compound Eyes. Compound eyes are by far the most important visual organs of insects. They occur in nearly all adult insects and in hemimetabolous larvae although they are reduced in size or absent in parasitic and cave-dwelling forms. Their large size and prominent situation, high on either side of the head, afford them a wide visual field in many directions. The compound eyes are so called because they consist of a large number of visual units built on

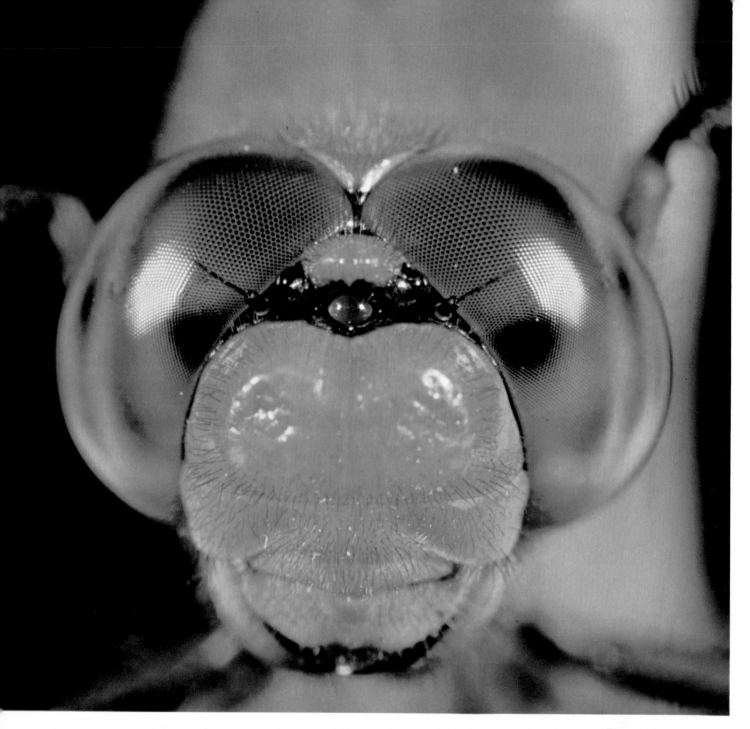

The head of the Green jacket dragonfly showing the high globular compound eyes consisting of several thousand ommatidia. As is frequently the case in dragonflies the facets in the upper part of the eye are much larger than those underneath. Also visible on the front of the head between the compound eyes are the three large dorsal ocelli.

the same plan as the stemmata of caterpillars. Each of these units, an ommatidium, typically has a cuticular lens, a cone-shaped crystalline lens and eight nerve cells. The nerve cells, or retinula cells, are elongate and are arranged in a rosette around the longitudinal axis of the ommatidium. The inner surfaces of the retinula cells form a rhabdom with

varying numbers of cells contributing to varying lengths of it in different insects. Each ommatidium is separated from its neighbours by a ring of cells containing pigment granules which absorb light. This is not the visual pigment, which is contained in the rhabdom, but instead is a screening pigment which optically isolates each ommatidium from all the others.

The number of ommatidia in each compound eye varies from one, in the worker of the ant *Ponera punctatissima*, to 10,000–28,000 in the huge globular eyes of the larger dragonflies. Where there are relatively few ommatidia, as in aphids, the cuticular lenses or facets are round in surface view and separated from each other by normal cuticle. In the larger eyes, which are more compact, the numerous facets are packed closely together in a hexagonal array, like a miniature honeycomb. The size of ommatidia varies between insects and sometimes within the same eye; in some dragonflies the dorsal facets are twice as large as the ventral ones. In males of the fly *Bibio* the regions of large and small facets are sharply divided and this is carried further in males of the mayfly *Cloëon*, where the two regions of each eye are quite separate, giving the insect the grotesque appearance of having four large and slightly stalked eyes. The eyes are similarly divided in the water beetle *Gyrinis* so that, as it swims on the surface, the dorsal part of the eye surveys the aerial world, while the ventral part is below the water-line and monitors events there.

Apposition and Superposition Eyes. The main lens of the ommatidium is the crystalline cone and this forms a small, erect image of its field of view. As in the stemmata, however, this bears no relationship to what the insect actually sees because there are too few sensory cells in a single ommatidium to split up the image into its details and record each separately. Instead, it is believed that each ommatidium registers the average light intensity of that part of the visual field which it faces. The overall impression from the whole eye is of a series of dots of light of different intensities. Taken together, they form a mosaic image of the visual field similar, but opposite, to that of a newspaper photograph which is made by printing black dots of varying sizes on white paper. This mosaic theory of insect vision was first proposed as long ago as 1829 by Johannes Müller and has been challenged in various ways since then. It appears, for example, that each ommatidium receives light from an angle as wide as $20°$. This means that the fields of adjacent ommatidia overlap to a great extent and they would all therefore report much the same light intensity. However, it has since been shown that the amount of light getting through the ommatidial lens system is greatly reduced as the angle widens, so that each ommatidium effectively looks at only a small part of the visual field. With an effective ommatidial angle of $4°$, an insect will receive only one spot of light from an object which it would be able to resolve into 16 spots with an ommatidial angle of $1°$. The screening pigment also ensures that each ommatidium is stimulated only by that light which entered its own lens system; any stray light which might

affect an adjacent ommatidium is absorbed. Images thus formed by the apposition of adjacent spots of light are known as apposition images, and compound eyes functioning this way, as apposition eyes. This is the normal type of eye found in diurnal insects.

In many nocturnal insects the situation is rather different. Here the screening pigment moves within the cells and the cells themselves can migrate to a certain extent. In bright light, the pigment extends between the ommatidia as in an apposition eye, but in dim light the pigment withdraws towards the outer surface of the eye so that the groups of retinula cells are no longer screened from each other and light can pass through the cells from one ommatidium to another. Whereas, in the apposition eye, each lens forms a tiny image near the base of the crystalline cone, in this type of eye, these images spread and superimpose on each other deeper in the eye. In this, the superposition eye, the retinula cells respond to the varying intensities at different points in the superposition image. This image is undoubtedly less sharply defined than that produced by an apposition eye because the superimposing images are not quite congruent, but less light is wasted by being absorbed by screening pigment. These insects, which include many moths and beetles, form apposition images in bright light but superposition images when low light intensity is a limiting factor. Light is further conserved in some moths by the presence around the inner ends of the retinula cells of many small tracheae. These form a mirror or 'tapetum' at the back of the eye and reflect light back through the ommatidia again, giving it a second chance to be absorbed by visual pigment in the rhabdoms. These moths, caught in the light from a car's headlamps, show glowing eyes like those of cats and other mammals with a comparable tapetum.

Recently another type of superposition image has been discovered. Due to diffraction of light by the lenses of groups of ommatidia acting together, a series of diffraction images are formed at progressively greater depths in the eye. Some of these fall in the rhabdom region and could give visual information, especially of objects with radial symmetry which readily form diffraction images, but the details are not yet understood. Much doubt has been expressed as to whether any type of superposition images could ever be formed, as the internal tissue of the eye may not be sufficiently transparent or homogeneous for the light to pass through coherently.

That these doubts are unfounded has recently been neatly shown using the eye of the moth *Ephestia*. The V-shaped filament of a light bulb was viewed with a microscope focussing through the eye of the moth from the inside. When focussed on the base of the crystalline cones, the microscope revealed a series of V-shaped images in hexagonal array. Focussing the microscope back through the retinula cells caused the images to enlarge and finally to overlap and fuse into a single image – the superposition image.

The visual pigment in insects is a chemical known as rhodopsin. This consists of retinal, a form of vitamin A, linked with a protein. Thus rhodopsin belongs to a group of chemicals called chromo-proteins. The wavelength at which the pigment absorbs maximally is dependent on the structure of the protein. The rhodopsin, thought to be situated in the microvilli of the rhabdom, is bleached by light and the retinal and protein dissociate. This process somehow causes electrical changes in the cell which, if large enough, result in nerve impulses being transmitted to the brain. The visual pigment is continuously resynthesized.

Perception of Form, Movement and Distance. It is difficult to compare the efficiency of insect eyes with that of our own. Photographs of objects taken through the eye of the glow-worm *Lampyris* indicate that the resolving power of the insect eye is about one seventieth that of the human eye but behavioural experiments suggest that the resolving power in the bee *Apis* is one hundredth, and in the fruit-fly *Drosophila* one thousandth, of that of man.

If an insect is placed on the floor of a cylindrical drum, whose inner walls have vertical black and white stripes, and the patterned walls are made to rotate with respect to the floor, the insect will turn

Honey bees *Apis* alighting on the platform on the entrance to their hive after foraging flights. With their compound eyes, these insects are able to distinguish the colours of flowers and other objects and also to recognize and respond to the shapes which are commonly associated with flowers. Additionally they can detect plane of polarization and hence navigate by the position of the sun even when it is behind clouds.

with the pattern so keeping it more or less stationary with respect to its eyes. This 'optomotor' reaction can be used to investigate the acuity of vision by substituting a pattern of narrower stripes until the insect can no longer distinguish them and indicates this by failing to rotate with the pattern. Thus tested, most insects are found to be capable of distinguishing objects with an angular separation of 1 or 2°.

Most phytophagous insects respond readily to vertical stripe patterns and often move towards the black/white boundaries. This is probably related to the common habit in these insects of feeding on the edges of leaves. Bees and ants recognize the patterns of landmarks in finding their way back to the nest. The ability of the honey-bee *Apis* to respond to different shapes has been tested by training bees to associate a particular shape with the presence of food. Subsequently, in the absence of food, the bees

A Bush cricket eating the leaf of a plant of the rose family. Notice the large compound eyes high on each side of the head, well placed to monitor the surrounding environment and give early warning of any danger.

are offered this shape in competition with others and the percentage choosing the original shape is noted. Solid shapes are not differentiated from each other, nor are broken ones, but the bees easily differentiate between solid and broken ones and broken shapes may be chosen even when the bees have been trained to a solid one. Bees, like butterflies, show a natural preference for broken patterns such as those displayed by flowers, especially when the flowers are vibrating in the wind. They probably associate such a flickering appearance with the presence of nectar so that the experiments with solid shapes perhaps do not give a true estimate of the insect's ability to distinguish shapes. The number of visits paid by bees to any pattern is proportional to the length of its contour. This suggests that an important factor is the frequency with which contours pass across the ommatidial fields as the insect moves.

The insect eye is well suited to the perception of movement. Because of the large number of ommatidia, small movements of objects, or of the eyes, cause changes in stimulation as the light intensity on ommatidia alters. If this flicker effect is too rapid, the vibration of an object may go unnoticed because the sensory units need time to recover between stimulations. The frequency at which this occurs, the flicker fusion frequency, is, in general, low in slow moving insects but high in fast fliers. A high flicker threshold enables fast flying insects to distinguish features of the ground and vegetation passing rapidly by.

An important feature of compound eyes is that they allow insects to judge distance accurately. This requires binocular vision – it cannot be done with one eye covered over. As a dragonfly larva approaches a potential prey, the image of the prey on the retinas of the two eyes moves towards the midline of the insect. The larva knows by experience just where on the retinas the image should be when the prey can be seized. The accuracy of the estimate is increased with a longer baseline between the predator's eyes. Thus many visual predators such as mantids and Zygoptera have broad heads with eyes as far apart as possible. Grasshoppers, which need to judge their jumps accurately, increase the effective baseline by making lateral peering movements at a proposed perch.

Polarized Light and Colour Vision. Light coming from the sky vibrates in some planes more than others and the plane of maximum polarization is related to the position of the sun. Many insects are able to detect the plane of polarization and it is thought that the microvilli of the rhabdomeres act as polarization filters, but the plane of polarization can also be detected by some ocelli and stemmata. This ability is used by ants and honey-bees in their navigation.

Species of most of the major orders of insects are capable of colour vision and this is particularly so of flower-visiting species such as bees and butterflies. Different visual pigments respond differentially to different wavelengths of light. Studies with the electron microscope indicate that these different pigments reside in the microvilli of different retinula cells in the honey-bee *Apis*. Much behavioural work has been carried out on this species and it is well established that the honey-bee has a trichromatic system like our own, but having blue, yellow and ultraviolet as the primary colours. Unlike us, insects see well in ultraviolet but not in the red end of the spectrum. The red flowers of poppies are seen by insects mainly by patterns of ultraviolet light reflected from them which are invisible to us, while we see the red which the insect does not.

Mechanical and Chemical Senses

We have seen how the cuticle over the eyes of insects is not only transparent to allow the entry of an external stimulus, but, in being lens shaped, may modify that stimulus so that it can more readily be detected by the sensory cells beneath. Similarly, the otherwise insensitive cuticle may be modified in other parts of the body to serve in the detection of the energy associated with other types of stimulus. The most obvious of these cuticular modifications are the bristles which are scattered all over the body of most insects, but there are many other cuticular structures which mediate the mechanical and chemical senses and are known collectively as sensilla – that is, little sense organs.

Trichoid Sensilla. Some of the bristles on an insect's body are stiff and insensitive, but most are moveably inserted into a basal socket and associated with a nerve cell. Each sensillum is formed by an epidermal cell which gives up its normal function of cuticle production and, by division, gives rise to a cell which produces the elongate cuticular cone of the hair, another which produces the socket, and a third which becomes the nerve cell. This last cell, lying in the epidermis beneath the sensillum, extends

This picture of a beetle shows that most of the surface of an insect is covered with minute bristles. Their main function is to trigger off sense cells inside the body when they are stimulated by changes in the outside environment.

a sensitive projection, the dendrite, into the hair, and another, longer projection, the axon, grows through the internal tissue, often with others of its kind, forming a nerve, to join the central nervous system. When the hair is moved by contact with some object, it acts as a lever to deform the end of the dendrite lying at its base. This causes a change in the electrical charge always present in the dendrite, which in turn results in pulses of electricity, of standard size, being transmitted along the axon to the brain. The frequency of these impulses is determined by the size of the electrical change produced in the dendrite, and that in turn by the extent to which the hair was moved. Thus information about the external event is now coded in the frequency of pulses reaching the central nervous system and somehow the animal knows whether the otherwise identical impulses signal touch, temperature, humidity, taste, depending on the type of organ from which they originate.

In some of these sensilla, the dendrites function in such a way that impulses are transmitted only when the hair is actually moving. Such sensilla function as touch receptors and occur particularly on the tarsi,

antennae, mouthparts and indeed on any part of the body with which the insect touches the substratum. Insects, like the cockroach, are using these sensilla as they ceaselessly explore their surroundings with long, supple antennae.

These tactile sensilla may be sufficiently sensitive to respond to vibrations carried in the substratum or even to the slight air movements caused by sound waves. Hairs on the body of some caterpillars detect sound waves in the range of 30–1,000 cycles per second and this results in convulsive writhing movements by the caterpillar if the sound is loud enough. If the hairs are shaved off or loaded with powder, the caterpillar no longer responds. The tail filaments, or cerci, of grasshoppers and cockroaches bear similar hairs and those of *Periplaneta* respond to sound waves up to 3,000 cycles per second. When these hairs are stimulated by a puff of air, the cockroach takes rapid evasive action.

Another type of trichoid mechanoreceptor sensillum produces a response all the time and not only when the hair is moving. In these sensilla the output varies with the position of the hairs. They are often grouped together in hair beds and situated at joints in the body and legs and are stimulated differentially by varying degrees of flexion of the joints. That is, they give the insect information about the disposition of its body and are therefore involved in 'self-perception' or proprioception as it is called. The use of these position receptors has been investigated in prey capture by mantids. We saw in the previous chapter how a dragonfly larva would strike at a prey with its labial mask when the compound eyes indicated that the prey was within reach. Mantids also rely on this visual information but the prey is seized with the forelegs which, of course, are attached to the thorax and not to the head as is the dragonfly's labial mask. The mantid always turns its head to look directly at the prey and it must therefore know how far it has turned its head in order to know to what extent the legs should strike sideways from the front of the thorax. The strike is made in 10–30 milliseconds, so there is no chance of the mantid watching the stroke and correcting its direction as it proceeds; the legs must flash out in exactly the direction in which the head is facing. The necessary information is obtained from hair beds on the neck touching the back of the head at either side. As the head turns to the right, the hairs on the right are bent more and those on the left less, with corresponding increase and decrease in nervous output. With intact hair beds the accuracy of

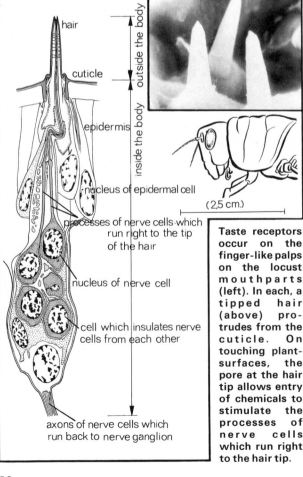

hair

cuticle

outside the body

inside the body

epidermis

nucleus of epidermal cell

processes of nerve cells which run right to the tip of the hair

nucleus of nerve cell

cell which insulates nerve cells from each other

axons of nerve cells which run back to nerve ganglion

(2.5 cm.)

Taste receptors occur on the finger-like palps on the locust mouthparts (left). In each, a tipped hair (above) protrudes from the cuticle. On touching plant-surfaces, the pore at the hair tip allows entry of chemicals to stimulate the processes of nerve cells which run right to the hair tip.

The fly *Delia antiqua* clearly shows the many bristles which project all over the insect's body. Most of these are sensitive to touch and some are also sensitive to taste.

striking is about 85 %. When information from both beds is blocked, the success rate falls to 20–30 %. When the right side only is blocked, the rate of missing is even higher and there is a tendency to strike too far to the left. That is, information coming from the left side only makes the animal believe that its head is turned further to the left than it actually is.

By means of similar hair beds, the honey-bee *Apis* learns of its position in relation to gravity; information which it uses in its communication dances performed on the vertical comb of its dark hive. These hair beds are so positioned that when the bee stands on a horizontal surface, the hairs on both sides of the head are stimulated equally. However, the centre of gravity of the head lies below the point of articulation with the thorax so that the head tends to nod down when the bee crawls up a vertical surface and to loll to the side if it crawls at an angle to the vertical. Thus from the differential stimulation of these hair beds, the insect gets a measure of its orientation with respect to gravity.

A rather different use is made of hair beds which occur on the face of the locust. These hairs respond to air blowing onto the face at speeds of greater than 6·5 ft (2 m) per second. Their response is dependent on wind direction so that they enable the insect to orientate to the wind while on the ground and while in flight, where they are also concerned in the control of yaw.

Campaniform Sensilla. Possibly a modified form of the trichoid sensillum, these campaniform or bell-shaped organs occur on practically all parts of the body. They lack the tactile hair, which is replaced by an oval, domed cap of cuticle. This cap is susceptible to distortion in its long axis by stresses in the cuticle and it is this distortion which stretches the dendrite and results in the production of nerve impulses, whose frequency is related to the degree of distortion. These sensilla are concentrated particularly where stresses are set up in the cuticle by muscular contraction, that is, adjacent to the joints of legs, wings, halteres, ovipositors and mouth parts. They often occur in groups, all those within a group having the same orientation, but often differing in size, which perhaps gives them a range of sensitivity. Their continuous nervous output, related to degree of stress, enables them to act as proprioreceptors monitoring the activity of whole limbs.

Chordotonal Organs. A further reduction in the cuticular elements of the sensillum may have been

81

responsible for the development of chordotonal organs. These cord-like organs, often invisible from the outside, consist of a variable number of units which together form a strand of tissue suspended between points on the cuticle. The essential part of each unit is a nerve cell whose dendrite is stretched by movements of the cuticle. They occur throughout the body of the insect and particularly in the legs where they act as proprioreceptors, giving information about the position of joints, but also responding to external disturbances.

There are typically four chordotonal organs in each leg of many insects. Of these, three are associated with joints and are proprioceptors, but the fourth, the subgenual organ, which is suspended in the proximal part of the tibia, is not associated with a joint and is often very sensitive to vibrations. In the cockroach *Periplaneta* for instance, this organ is sensitive to displacements of as little as 10^{-9}–10^{-7} cm and to frequencies up to 8,000 cycles per second. The cockroach, therefore, is very alert to disturbances in its vicinity which cause vibrations, including high frequency transients, to be transmitted through the substratum.

Movements of the antennae are monitored by a group of chordotonal organs at the joint between the second antennal segment and the rest of the antenna. This group, called Johnston's organ, is to be found in virtually all adult insects and in many larvae as well. Apart from giving general proprioceptive information about the antennae, it has developed as an air speed indicator in some insects and as an organ of hearing and direction location in others.

The cockroach is well equipped with long sensory hairs on its legs. The antennae, which are very long and flexible bear numerous touch-sensitive hairs as well as a variety of organs sensitive to smell. The antennae-like organs, or cerci, at the tail end are also very sensitive.

In flight, the blowfly *Calliphora* experiences a wind on its face, the strength of which is proportional to the speed at which the insect flies through the air. This wind causes a bristle called an arista to act as a lever and rotate the third antennal segment on the second, so stimulating Johnston's organ to an extent proportional to the air speed of the flying insect. Apart from registering air speed, this organ is used in monitoring and controlling flight activity. If the antennae of an aphid are cut off beyond the second segment, the flight is erratic, but normal flight capability is restored if artificial antennae are stuck on.

Johnston's organ is used in navigation and orientation in some aquatic insects. The beetle *Gyrinus* swims with its antennae in the surface film and, by means of Johnston's organ, is able to detect curves in the surface near objects and so avoid collisions. It is also said to be able to echolocate objects which reflect its own ripples. The bug *Notonecta* (Heteroptera) swims under water on its back and carries an air bubble between the antennae and the head. The buoyancy of the air bubble pushes the antennae away from the head but if the insect gets the wrong way up, the antennae lie closer to the head and this situation is registered by Johnston's organ.

The most elaborate development of Johnston's organ occurs in the males of chironomid midges and mosquitoes (Culicidae). The second antennal segment is swollen and bulbous to house the organ and the rest of the antenna bears numerous long hairs arising from each joint. The whole hairy antenna is caused to vibrate by sound waves and this stimulates Johnston's organ. The amplitude of vibration is greatest at the natural frequency of the antenna which is about 500 cycles per second. This is also the wingbeat frequency of mature females, and males fly towards such a sound. The individual units of the Johnston's organ are so arranged that the male can detect the direction from which sounds reaching his antennae have come. Stimulation at the appropriate frequency leads to the clasping response in mating, and males have been known to attempt to copulate with a tuning fork kept vibrating at the right frequency. The frequency range to which a male responds gets wider as the insect gets older, and wider still if it has never mated.

Tympanal Organs. A different sort of specialization of chordotonal organs to allow sound detection of a wider frequency range occurs in tympanal organs. The chordotonal organs are attached at one end to a thin cuticular membrane, the tympanum,

A nymph of the locust *Schistocerca*. There are beds of sensory hairs on the front of the head, between the antennae, which respond to wind blowing on the face. Their response is directional so that the locust can orientate to the wind.

which is set in the body surface and, backed by air sacs, is free to vibrate at the frequency of the sound waves impinging upon it. There is usually one organ on each side of the body, at the back of the thorax or front of the abdomen, as in some aquatic bugs and moths, cicadas (Homoptera) and grasshoppers and locusts (Acrididae). Tympanal organs also occur on the tibia of the fore legs in crickets (Gryllidae) and bush crickets (Tettigonidae).

These organs detect the displacement of air particles, rather than the changes in pressure, associated with sound waves and therefore show directional sensitivity. The response is maximal when sound waves strike the tympanum at right angles to its surface, and falls off rapidly on either side of this. A Tettigonid searches for a sound source by swinging its fore legs around till it gets a suddenly increased pulse of sound as the tympanum faces the source.

Similarly, flying moths can locate a sound source in the horizontal plane on the basis of asymmetrical stimulation of the two tympani, one being more shielded by the body than the other. A flying insect must also locate sound in the vertical plane and here cyclical screening of the tympani by the wings may help. During a down beat, sounds from below will appear louder than those from above and will appear to increase in intensity as the wings form an increasingly effective reflector.

The principle known function of tympanal organs of moths is the detection of the hunting cries of bats which are predators on the moths. The frequency range of the moth's tympanal organ corresponds well with that of the bat's cry and its mode of response suits it well to register the short, rapidly repeated pulses of high frequency sound emitted by the bat. Moths can detect bats at a distance of 100 ft (30 m) or more and fly away from the low intensity sound they receive at that range. As the bat closes in, it increases the frequency of sound pulses emitted until at some critical level, when the bat is about 20 ft (7 m) away, the moth takes violent evasive action, closing its wings and dropping to the ground or even power diving into the vegetation. Despite its obvious dangers, this avoiding action does have survival value for the moth.

In the acridids and cicadas the auditory organs are used to detect and localize sound signals which are produced by other insects of the same species and, as

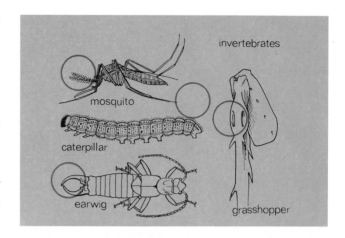

Insects use various modifications of their hard exoskeleton for the reception of sounds by the displacement of various structures.

we shall see later, have significance in mating and other behaviour.

Stretch Receptors. Stretch receptors are similar to chordotonal organs in having no external indication of their presence but differ from them, and from all other insect sense organs, in having several free nerve endings to each neurone rather than the usual single dendrite. They occur in connective tissue, often associated with muscle, and are commonly

A male mosquito showing the large, hairy antennae which are used as organs of hearing. The antennae of the male vibrate readily in response to the sound of the female wing-beats.

A mole cricket. In this subterranean insect, males sing loudly at certain times of the year, particularly at night. Their song is produced by vibration of the short wings as they are rubbed across each other.

found between adjacent segments of the abdomen where they monitor the degree of extension or telescoping of abdominal segments and the rhythmic movements associated with respiratory ventilation.

Orientation Receptors. Orientation with respect to gravity may be achieved by means of hair beds as already described, but occasionally statocysts are involved. This type of organ is very common in crustaceans but very rare in insects. The best known example occurs in *Dorymyrmex* (Hymenoptera) which has a cavity on the side of the metathorax just above the base of the leg. The cavity is lined with tactile hairs and contains one or two sand grains loosely supported by cuticular projections. As the insect alters its orientation with respect to gravity, the sand grains move and stimulate different hairs.

In some aquatic insects, determination of water pressure as a guide to depth is important. The bug *Aphelocheirus* (Heteroptera) is not buoyant and must swim to avoid resting on the bottom. It obtains oxygen from the water by means of a plastron system which functions efficiently only in oxygen-

rich water such as occurs near the surface, so that it benefits from being able to gauge its depth in the water. The organ concerned is a group of hairs, some of which are sensory, enclosed in a bubble of air on the under surface of the abdomen. As depth increases, the increasing pressure reduces the volume of air and the hairs inside the bubble are bent over, so registering the change.

A similar system operates in the water scorpion *Nepa* (Heteroptera) where the organs on three abdominal segments are interconnected internally by the tracheal system whose spiracles open into the air bubbles. When the insect dives the pressure difference between the foremost and deeper organ and the hindmost, shallower, organ is registered.

Chemoreception. Sensitivity of receptor cells to stimulation by chemicals produces the sensations which we call taste and smell. Although we may have a clear enough impression of the distinction between taste and smell, we are not always strictly accurate or consistent in making that distinction. For example, we taste chemicals in solution with our mouths and smell gaseous chemicals with our noses yet often

A Bush cricket with its elytra, or fore wings, raised to make the chirping sound characteristic of these insects. These sound signals are received by other members of the same species by means of tympanal organs situated in the fore legs.

when we relish the taste or flavour of a food we are basing our impression not only on the true taste, detected by receptors on the tongue, but also on the complex odours of the food being monitored at the same time by our noses. In insects, the distinction is more difficult because the antennae, the main organs of smell, also bear taste receptors, whilst the mouth parts, the main organs of taste, bear receptors responsive to odours. Similarly, insects can taste, and perhaps smell too, with such unlikely organs as their feet and their ovipositors and in aquatic insects, the chemicals of both taste and smell reach the insect dissolved in water. Despite these complications, it is useful to recognize two basic types of chemoreception in insects: olfaction, which is the detection of low concentrations of molecules in the gaseous state by fairly sensitive receptors, and gustation, which is the detection of higher concentrations of molecules in solution by less sensitive receptors.

One of the most common types of sensillum used is trichoid and similar in form to the hair-like sensilla which function as mechanoreceptors. Each trichoid chemoreceptor has several neurones whose dendrites extend into the hair which has holes in it

whereby the sensitive tips of the dendrites are exposed to the outside world. In taste organs, or contact chemoreceptors, there are four to six neurones and a single pore right at the tip of the hair. Receptors of this sort occur on almost all parts of the insect which commonly touch the substratum and are particularly numerous on the mouthparts where they monitor the quality of the food about to be ingested. Olfactory receptors of the trichoid type have from 10–50 neurones and the hair has thin walls with numerous pores like a colander, so increasing the exposure of dendrites to the odour molecules. These sensilla sometimes occur on the mouthparts but are most common on the antennae where they are sometimes present in large numbers in sunken pits which may protect their fragile walls.

As with mechanoreceptors, forms have evolved in which the hair is reduced or absent. Thus inside the mouth cavity of locusts and grasshoppers are to be found groups of taste receptors which look like very small pimples, each with a hole at the top through which the four or five dendrites are exposed. These sensilla taste the fluid squeezed out of plants by the jaws. Olfactory sensilla with reduced hairs occur on the antennae of aphids, bees and others. They are known as plate organs and the numerous dendrites are exposed through a multitude of pores in a flat oval disc of thin cuticle slightly raised above the level of the general cuticle.

The processes whereby chemicals stimulate the dendrites of these receptors are very poorly understood but it is assumed that the chemical reacts with the dendritic membrane for a short time in such a way as to produce a change in its electrical properties. This change soon dies away but if it is reinforced by a succession of molecules it results in the transmission of information to the brain. The fewer molecules needed to achieve this, the more sensitive the receptor. An extremely sensitive receptor on the antennae of the adult male Silkmoth *Bombyx mori* responds to a single molecule of the female sex pheromone.

If the dendritic membranes of different neurones responded to different chemicals, and each to only one chemical, then the insect would have a ready means of identifying chemicals. There is no good evidence to suggest that this degree of specificity ever occurs but certainly examples do exist of specialist neurones which respond very readily to a particular compound of significance to the insect and very little to any other chemicals. This sort of specificity may be shown by an olfactory receptor towards a

A Water scorpion, a bug of the order Heteroptera. This aquatic insect orientates in water by detecting pressure differences by means of special organs associated with spiracles on three abdominal segments. The long pointed organ at the top of the abdomen is a breathing tube.

component of the sex pheromone or by a gustatory receptor towards a particular component of a favoured food. The more common, generalist, receptors respond to a number of compounds, which usually have some chemical affinity with each other. Many olfactory receptors are of the specialist type, for example the antennae of males of the moth *Telea polyphemus* bear 60,000 sensilla having 150,000 receptor cells of which 60–70 % are specialists responding to the female sex pheromone of that species, while the remaining 30 % are generalists responding differentially to a wide range of odours. It has been thought for many years that taste sensilla, such as those on the feet and mouth-parts of blowflies, had neurones of the specialist type responding more or less exclusively to salt or sugar or water. Recently however, experiments have shown that while individual neurones may respond best to one of these compounds, they usually are able to respond to very many others as well.

Investigations of chemoreception in insects involve behavioural and neurophysiological experiments. Excellent subjects for study are the taste sensilla on the tarsi of blowflies and butterflies. When these sensilla are brought into contact with a

substance which the insect 'likes', such as sweetened water, the proboscis is immediately extended in search of the food, but if the substance is 'disliked', the proboscis is withdrawn. The response is very obvious and leaves the investigator in no doubt of the insect's reaction. In this way a wide range of soluble substances may be tested in different concentrations and different combinations. These investigations are carried out in conjunction with neurophysiology in which the nerve impulses generated in the chemoreceptors are recorded. A metal electrode, less than one millionth of a metre in diameter, is gently inserted into the side of the hair and a test solution brought into contact with the hole at the tip. The impulses are then amplified thousands of times before being studied. Similar techniques may be employed to record from olfactory sensilla in an intact insect and to check behavioural responses to olfactory stimuli.

Behavioural experiments indicate that many insects are sensitive to humidity but it has proved very difficult to identify the receptors involved. In most cases the antennae seem to be concerned. In the beetle *Tenebrio* the responses to humidity are reduced progressively as more of the antennal surface is covered but there do not appear to be any special

Lepidoptera often have very sensitive organs of smell: this photograph clearly shows the antennae of *Platysamia cercropia* which bear the scent receptors. Each side branch of the antennae carries numerous hair-like sense organs each of which has many nerve cells sensitive to odours important in the insect's life.

A human body louse clinging to a strand of hair. Apart from many other types of sense organs, these insects have minute tufts of branched hairs on the antennae. By means of these hairs the insect detects and responds to changes in humidity.

receptors and it is thought that the normal trichoid olfactory sensilla are involved. In a flour beetle *Tribolium*, however, there are branched hairs on the antennae, and in the louse *Pediculus* there are tufts of four to six minute hairs near the tips of the antennae. In both cases, when these organs are covered with cellulose paint, the animal no longer responds to changes in humidity. The mode of functioning of these sensilla is equally obscure, and has as yet escaped elucidation.

Among the most important sense organs in insects are the antennae seen in the ladybird to the left of this picture. The pair have been photographed during copulation, a subject that is discussed in the next chapter.

Reproduction

The culmination of the life history of an insect occurs in reproduction and the principal behavioural patterns of an insect, apart from those associated with survival itself, are directed towards achieving reproductive success. Insects reproduce sexually; a female cell, the ovum, fuses with, and is thereby fertilized by, a male cell, the sperm. These sex cells, or gametes, are produced in the paired sex organs situated in the abdomen of the adult insect; the ovaries in the female and the testes in the male. In the course of its development, the nucleus of each gamete comes to contain only half of the normal number of chromosomes for that species. These chromosomes determine the hereditary characteristics of the insect and the full complement is restored on fertilization; half from the male and half from the female. Thus when the fertilized egg subsequently divides into many cells which develop in different ways to form the many parts of a new insect, that insect can express the various characteristics inherited from each of the two parents.

The Reproductive System. The female reproductive system consists of a pair of ovaries lying laterally above the gut in the abdomen and connected by tubes to the exterior. Each ovary consists of a series of tubes, at the upper ends of which the eggs are produced. The number of tubes, or ovarioles, in each ovary varies from one in the tsetse fly to 2,000 in some queen termites. As the eggs move singly along the length of each ovariole they receive a supply of yolk and finally shell. The eggs from each ovary pass into a common median oviduct and via the vagina to the exterior. Another tube opening into the vagina leads to a sac, the spermatheca, used for the storage of sperm collected during copulation, and often a pair of accessory glands also discharge into the vagina. The accessory glands produce a sticky material which cements the eggs to the substrate or holds them together in masses.

For the development of eggs, or oogenesis, to occur, the insect must be mature and the process is controlled by hormones from the brain. Apart from this, environmental conditions such as temperature and day length may have an effect, acting via the hormonal system. Adequate nutrition is also important; in the absence of sufficient food, many insects fail to produce eggs or resorb those already developing in the ovarioles. Many mosquitoes, which can live for a long time on sugars, require a blood meal before they can produce eggs. In the desert locust *Schistocerca* the presence of mature males accelerates the production of eggs.

The male reproductive system is basically very similar to that of the female. The paired testes consist of many tubes along which the developing male gametes pass, to emerge in vast numbers as motile sperms equipped with long, mobile tails to drive the head which contains the nucleus. The mature sperm is stored in a quiescent state in the tubes from the testes which may be long or dilated for the purpose. These storage regions or seminal vesicles unite to form an ejaculatory duct leading to the external male organ, or penis. There are also accessory glands which discharge into the ejaculatory duct. In some insects the sperms are produced and released in packets called spermatophores which are produced by proteinaceous secretions of the accessory glands. It is thought that this technique may have evolved as the ancestors of insects became adapted to a terrestrial life. Most primitive aquatic animals discharge their sex cells into the water, but such release of sperms on land would result in their drying up. In the primitive insects of today, the Thysanura and Collembola, males distribute their spermatophores at random and some are encountered by females and taken into their genital openings. In more advanced insects, the spermatophores are inserted into the vagina of the female, while, in the higher orders, spermatophores are thought to be absent and sperms are inserted directly into the female genital aperture.

Courtship Behaviour. In order that sperm may be transferred from one individual to another it is necessary that the two should be brought together; some form of aggregation signal must be used. Usually some further signals are employed which enable the insects to recognize their own species and to determine each other's sex. Additionally it may be necessary for a male to employ tactics to stimulate an apparently coy and reluctant female, or alternatively to distract with food a female who would otherwise regard him as food. The production of the signals and the reactions to them constitute court-ship behaviour.

The signals used by courting insects may involve vision, sound or scent and the nature and use of such signals is considered in more detail later; we shall consider here the results of their use. Sounds, scent or sight causing the aggregation of insects may bring together a single male and female or may result in the accumulation of large numbers of either or both sexes. Apart from signals emitted by the insects themselves, swarming behaviour, in which a group of insects remains flying over one spot, may result from a reaction to some feature of the environment. Such are the swarms of small flies, common at sunset, holding station a few feet above a rock or a cow pat or under the tip of a branch silhouetted against the sky. The marker is a feature which contrasts with its background; in the fly *Culicoides nubeculosus* it is a dark area, such as damp sand, against a light background, but in *C. riethi* this is reversed and a light patch is chosen. These swarms are usually of one species only and usually consist of males only, but in some Diptera mixed swarms occur and in a few mosquitoes wholly female, as well as male, swarms are found. Commonly mating is seen to occur in or near the swarms but in some cases mating has never been observed at all in the swarms.

Once insects have come together, other signals are used to aid recognition of species and sex. When female mosquitoes fly into male swarms, they are recognized by the sound of their wing beat frequency. The male of the solitary bee *Andrena* is attracted to the nest area by smell, but the sight of the orange legs of the female is important in his final recognition of her. Although males seem able to recognize their own species fairly well, sex recognition is not always so accurate. The occurrence of males attempting to mate with other males is not uncommon, particularly when females are scarce. Sometimes the behaviour of an assaulted male mimics that of an unwilling female and a specific signal is used, such as a characteristic wing-flick in the fruit-fly *Drosophila*. More usually the mistaken male is simply kicked off.

This behaviour is similar to that shown by males where they are crowded together or where there is a shortage of females. Aggression between male crickets, using a special song as a 'weapon', is well known. A similar situation occurs in the sphecid wasp *Sphecius*. Males, which tend to become adult earlier than females, establish territories for themselves, driving off intruders of other species and fighting where necessary with males of their own species. The boundaries of these territories become learnt to some extent so that the amount of trespass and fighting is reduced as each male occupies his own territory for a week or so before the females arrive on the scene. As soon as a receptive female enters a territory the male chases her and mates with her. This territorial behaviour ensures that males are

A Green African praying mantis *Sphodromantis* female eats a brown male of the same species who has tried unsuccessfully to court her. This is not an uncommon outcome of courtship behaviour in mantids.

The Scorpion fly *Panorpa germanica*. Here the courtship behaviour of the male has failed to appease the predatory female. The female has overcome the hapless male and is proceeding to feed on him.

spread over a wide area, increasing the chances of a female encountering one, and reduces the likelihood of interference by other males during mating.

On some insects, such as the housefly *Musca*, mating follows immediately upon recognition but more frequently the otherwise receptive female will not accept the male immediately and some further courtship is required. It is suggested that this female coyness may be important in allowing further time for correct recognition and certainly, in some cases, a precise sequence of signals is exchanged between male and female. A more obvious significance of courtship is seen in species where the female is aggressive; courtship involves some form of appeasement by the male so that he is not attacked. The male scorpion fly *Panorpa* secretes drops of saliva which harden on the surface of a leaf. As the female eats them he copulates with her. The female mantid may eat the male and sometimes starts before copulation. The effect of eating his head is to induce copulatory behaviour by removing nervous inhibition from his brain. In some species of predaceous empid flies (Diptera), the male presents the female with a captive fly in a silk cocoon. The female feeds on the dead fly during copulation but drops it immediately afterwards. In other species this behaviour has become ritualized and the female is presented with a useless object, such as a petal

wrapped in a cocoon, or even an empty cocoon.

Strangely, courtship feeding also occurs in non-predatory species. In the bug *Stilbocoris*, which feeds on fig seeds, an adult male usually carries a seed impaled on his proboscis. This he will offer to a female, approaching her from behind but holding the seed so that she can see it, till it touches her antennae. By quivering his legs he vibrates the seed while injecting saliva into it, so making it more appetising. The female investigates the seed and if she inserts her proboscis into it to feed, the male closes in slowly till he can grasp her and copulate. Males which do not have a seed do not normally embark on courtship.

Mating and Insemination. In most insects, courtship behaviour results in the male and female coming together, one sex usually mounting on the back of the other, and the subsequent passage of sperm, either directly or in a spermatophore, into the reproductive apparatus of the female. In Collembola, however, males deposit spermatophores on the ground independently of females. In some species it is left to chance for a female to find one and insert it into her reproductive opening, but in other cases the male grasps the female by her antennae and leads her over the spermatophore. The spermatophores of *Campodea* (Thysanura) are also produced in the absence of a female and sperm can survive in them for two days. The male can produce about 200 in a week, but some of these will be eaten by himself and by other insects.

In the Pterygotes, spermatophores are passed directly from male to female. The penis, which is cuticular and often elaborate in form, engages with complimentary plates on the female and serves to hold the male and female genitalia together while the transfer is made. In gryllids and tettigonids (Orthoptera), the spermatophore is produced before the male meets a female and he will court only if he has one, but in other groups the spermatophore is formed during copulation. Immediately after the spermatophore is transferred, sperm migrate to the spermatheca where they are stored, sometimes for a long time, until they are needed to fertilize the eggs. Some species of the orders Heteroptera, Hymenoptera, Coleoptera, Diptera and others have dispensed with a spermatophore. Here the long, whip-like penis transfers the sperm directly into the female ducts and often right into the spermatheca.

In some blood-sucking bugs an unusual modification of the normal insemination process has occurred. In *Alloeorhynchus flavipes* a spine at the tip of the penis perforates the vaginal wall and the sperm are injected into the blood cavity. By some unknown means the sperm migrate to the ovaries where they penetrate the ovariole tubes to fertilize the eggs. In *Primicimex* the penis stabs the female on the top of the abdomen to inject sperm into the blood and in some other species a tissue connection has developed between the site of stabbing and the ovaries, along which the sperm make their way. Finally in *Anthocoris* there is a permanent opening, other than the reproductive one, through which the injection occurs. In all these cases, some sperm are digested by blood cells and it is thought that their nutritive value may prolong the survival of the females in the absence of a blood meal.

Oviposition. When mature, the eggs are propelled down the oviducts by waves of contraction and are deposited singly or in groups, depending on the

Top left: Scorpion flies *Panorpa communis* mating. The male has succeeded in appeasing the aggressive female and initiating copulation. Note how the female wing is held by the fold in the abdomen of the male. Below left: Poplar hawkmoths *Laothoe populi* mating. The genitalia of the two moths are locked together at the centre of the picture. This tail-to-tail orientation of the moths against a tree bark background produces almost a puzzle picture. Right: Damselflies *Calopteryx virgo* mating. The male transfers sperm to a pouch under the front of his abdomen, then grips the female behind the head with claspers at the tip of his abdomen. The female bends forward under him and slips the genitalia at the tip of her abdomen into his pouch to receive the sperm.

A Sloe bug *Dolycoris baccarum*, of Europe, with its batch of eggs stuck together and to the surface of a leaf. The eggs are laid on leaves of the Rose family, usually in batches of 28.

subsequent development of the immature insects that the oviposition site chosen by the female should afford the eggs adequate protection from the environment and that there should be an adequate supply of food available for the relatively immobile larvae. At the time of oviposition a change occurs in the pattern of behaviour of the adult female. This may simply involve flying around at dusk scattering eggs into damp grass as in some crane-flies (Diptera) but may alternatively involve an attraction, say to some odour, which was previously of no significance in her life but which characterizes the potential oviposition site. Thus female blowflies which previously responded to flowers on whose nectar they fed, are now attracted by the smell of carrion in which their larvae can develop. Similarly the braconid wasps which parasitize blowfly larvae are also attracted by the smell of carrion. They immerse themselves in the putrefying pulp of a decaying carcass, search out and oviposit in the writhing blowfly larvae and emerge exhausted and bedraggled to stagger off into the herbage. Similarly the fly *Orthellia* uses its ovipositor to form a cavity in the surface of a freshly deposited cow pat and lays a group of 25–35 eggs in it. Butterflies may be attracted to the leaves on which their larvae feed by the smell of the essential oils produced by the plant.

A South African ladybird *Chilomenes lunulata* laying her eggs. A sticky secretion applied to each egg sticks them to the leaf surface. The eggs are laid on the leaves of plants frequented by aphids, the food of the larval ladybirds.

species. Sometimes there is no particular structure involved in the deposition of eggs but often the tip of the abdomen or appendages on it are modified to form a tube or ovipositor. The ovipositor may be rigid but more usually can be folded away or telescoped when not in use. The ovipositor may be pointed or toothed so that eggs can be laid within the tissues of plant or animal hosts. Alternatively the eggs may be dropped passively, as in stick insects, or glued singly or in masses to some substrate. Some orthopterous insects deposit their eggs in packets or protective structures called oothecae. The protective case, secreted by the accessory glands, may be frothy as in the locust or cuticle-like as in cockroaches.

It is of great importance for the survival and

Left: An adult female ichneumon *Rhyssa persuasoria* showing the long hypodermic-like ovipositor with which she drills into tree trunks to oviposit in Wood wasp larvae. The position of the larvae is located by the smell of a fungus introduced into the trunk by the wood-boring wasp larvae. Top right: The pincushion effect of lacewing eggs. As soon as they hatch the larvae feed on the nearest insect food. It is suggested that were the eggs not on stalks, the first larvae to hatch would probably eat the remaining eggs. Bottom right: Larvae of an endoparasitic ichneumon emerging from a Small white butterfly caterpillar. When mature, the parasite larvae eat their way out through the skin of the dying host and spin their bright yellow cocoons in irregular masses on walls, stones or tree trunks.

The butterfly eggs are often laid on the underside of a leaf so that the eggs are not exposed unduly to heat and desiccation. The oviposition site may be very specific, as in some thrips (Thysanoptera) which can distinguish between the petals and the bracts of a particular flower species.

Many parasitic insects lay their eggs on or in the host but, in others, the female oviposits in an area frequented by the host. Trigonalids (Hymenoptera) are parasitic on ichneumons (Hymenoptera) which are themselves parasites of caterpillars (of Lepidoptera or sawflies). The trigonalid eggs are laid on leaves which must be eaten by a caterpillar infected by an ichneumon for the final host to be reached. This is clearly a wasteful process and each female trigonalid produces several thousand eggs. The eggs of the Human warble fly *Dermatobia* follow an equally devious route. Other insects, especially mosquitoes, are used to provide transport to the human host. The female warble fly waits at a pool and when an adult mosquito emerges from the pupa she captures it and lays up to 15 eggs on its abdomen.

Some aquatic insects lay their eggs on floating vegetation, others, like the mosquito *Culex*, land on the water and float their eggs on the surface. Some species lay their eggs under water; the female damselfly *Hetaerina* may remain submerged to a depth of 4–5 in (100–127 mm) for up to an hour while she lays her eggs on the roots of the willow, *Salix*. The beetle *Ilybius* makes incisions in aquatic vegetation to lay its eggs in the airspaces of the plant. The tiny myrmarid *Caraphractus* (Hymenoptera) swims under water in order to parasitize these eggs.

Unusual Types of Reproduction. Although, as we have seen, the standard pattern of reproduction in insects involves a male and female mating, and the production of fertilized eggs, which are then deposited in some suitable site and left to their own devices; there are many variations on this theme.

In some species, occurring in several orders and

95

Top: A female sawfly *Tenthredo mesomelas* photographed while laying her eggs in a grass stem. The name sawfly derives from the serrated ovipositor adapted for sawing or boring into plant stems or wood for egg laying. It is never used as a sting.

Egg masses of the mosquito *Culex*. The adult female lands on the water and sticks her eggs together to form a floating 'raft' on the surface of the water. In this view from above, the egg rafts are surrounded by newly hatched larvae.

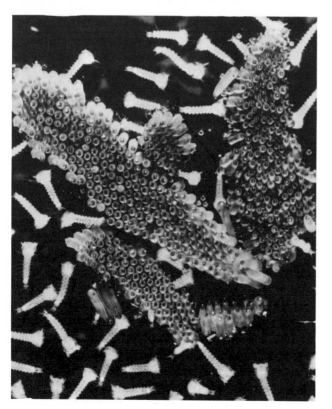

particularly in the Diptera, the fertilized eggs pass but slowly down through the reproductive tracts of the female so that the development of the embryo has started before the eggs are laid. Sometimes species of the fly *Musca*, which normally lay eggs, retain the eggs so long that they hatch as they are laid and larvae are deposited instead. In other flies this is the normal occurrence, a mode of reproduction known as viviparity. The flesh fly *Sarcophaga* can drop its larvae through the wire mesh of a meat safe on to the meat below. The Sheep bot fly *Oestrus ovis* hovers around the face of sheep and injects into the nostrils its larvae which continue their development in the face cavities of the unfortunate sheep. It is common for eggs which develop in this way to be larger than normal and to be produced in smaller numbers. The extra size is due to the presence of more yolk which may allow the embryo to develop beyond the normal hatching stage so that the larvae are born in a late stage of development. In the nests of some termites is to be found a strange fly called *Termitoxenia* whose large egg hatches immediately on laying, giving birth to a fully grown larva which pupates a few minutes later, so that the larva never feeds as a free-living insect.

In all these cases, the embryo or larva depends entirely on the yolk for its nourishment but this type of development has been taken a stage further by some insects. In *Hemimerus* (Dermaptera) the egg has virtually no yolk and no shell. It lies in close contact with special cells in the ovary from which it

96

derives food. But the most sophisticated development of this technique occurs in the tsetse fly *Glossina*. The egg develops in the usual way and hatches inside a 'uterus' formed from the enlarged vagina. Here the larva remains until it is fully grown and is nourished by special 'milk' glands which ramify throughout the abdomen. The 'milk' is delivered to the larva through a duct which opens on a tiny nipple on the 'uterus' wall, close to the mouth of the larva. Only one larva develops at a time and it breathes through a pair of modified spiracles pushed out through the vaginal opening. As it grows, the larva sheds its cuticle periodically and finally emerges, to pupate almost immediately. During her six months' adult life, the female tsetse produces about 12 larvae.

One of the most familiar examples of a viviparous insect is the aphid; the embryos develop so rapidly that the female may give birth to up to 12 young in 24 hours and become surrounded by a little flock of her offspring. But the aphids have another pec-

uliarity; they are often parthenogenetic, that is, the eggs develop without fertilization. Parthenogenesis, or virgin birth, occurs in many other insects besides the aphids. In the Common stick insect *Carausius morosus* it is the normal occurrence; males are extremely rare and when they do occur they are usually incapable of mating. Parthenogenesis allows reproduction to occur when males are absent or scarce, but is not so good for the population as sexual reproduction, because it does not allow the mixing of genetic material which may turn up new and useful combinations of inherited characters.

Some insects, like the aphids, combine the advantages of parthenogenesis with the advantages of sexual reproduction by an alternation of generations. In *Aphis fabae* there is an alternation of host plant too. In spring, the first generation of the year hatches from eggs which have overwintered on the spindle tree. This generation is entirely female and several further generations of wingless females are produced viviparously before a winged gen-

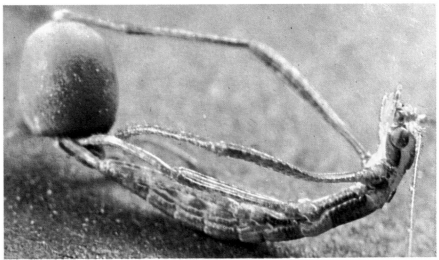

Stick insect *Carausius morosus* hatching. This species is often kept in insectaria and breeds parthenogenetically: males are very seldom found. The young insects emerge from the unfertilized eggs after some months by lifting a small lid. The empty egg-shell is often carried about for several days after birth.

eration appears. These winged females migrate to the summer food plants, mainly broad beans, where further wingless generations are produced. In autumn the shortening length of day influences the hormonal system and some winged females are produced which return to the spindle tree and in due course produce a generation of wingless females. The females remaining on the bean plants now produce winged males which fly to the spindle trees and mate with the wingless females already there. The now fertilized females proceed to produce eggs which remain on the spindle tree till the following spring, while all the adults die off.

The rate of reproduction of parthenogenetic female aphids in the summer is so rapid that development of the offspring of a female may start while that female is still herself developing in the reproductive ducts of her mother, thus successive generations are extensively telescoped. Although the young are not born till the aphid has become adult, development of the offspring continues through the larval life of the parent. This precocious maturation enabling an immature insect to reproduce is called paedogenesis and occurs in a number of insects in a number of ways. The female cecidomyid midge *Miastor* (Diptera) contains four or five very large eggs, in each of which a correspondingly large larva develops. Each of these produces paedogenetically from 7 to 30 daughter larvae which consume most of the tissues of the original female before eating their way out to reproduce on their own. When there is abundant food in the rotten tree stumps in which *Miastor* larvae occur, paedogenetic reproduction will occur indefinitely. Otherwise, after several generations of paedogenetic larvae, pupation occurs, resulting in male and female flies which may or may not give rise to another paedogenetic cycle. In other examples of paedogenetic reproduction larvae can give birth to eggs, or again pupae can give birth to eggs or to larvae. Paedogenesis usually occurs only under very good or very bad nutritional conditions.

Another variant on normal reproduction occurs

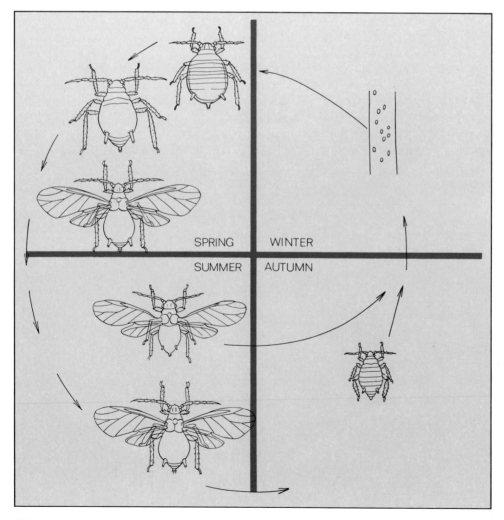

Life-history of aphids. Eggs (top right) hatch to give wingless females which reproduce parthenogenetically (top left). After several generations, wingless females (bottom right) are produced in autumn which mate with winged males (upper figure bottom left) and lay winter resistant eggs.

SPRING WINTER
SUMMER AUTUMN

A wingless female aphid giving birth parthenogenetically, that is, without prior fertilisation. Sometimes the eggs hatch before they are laid and young nymphs are born. In summer, when reproduction is rapid, another generation may be already developing inside the newly born young.

in some parasitic Hymenoptera which lay their eggs inside the body of another insect. This is the production of two or more larvae from a single egg and is called polyembryony. We have the same occurrence ourselves in the production of identical twins but the insects are usually much more prolific. In some chalcid wasps the embryo may split up to give a chain of about a hundred embryos and the highest claim is for as many as a thousand from a single egg.

A very rare method of diverging from normal sexual reproduction occurs in the scale insect *Icerya purchasi* (Homoptera). In the Californian race of this species, males are extremely rare and true females are unknown. All the individuals are hermaphrodites having the sex organs of both males and females. The testis is surrounded by the ovary and their anatomy is such that self-fertilization can occur. The hermaphrodites can be fertilized by the occasional males which develop from the few infertile eggs, but cross-fertilization between the hermaphrodites does not occur.

Growth and Development

The growth and development of an insect from embryo to adult encompasses a series of diverse and fascinating processes. The over-riding evolutionary pressure has been for the conquering of the terrestrial habitat. The solutions found to the many problems of this conquest, and the subsequent constraints these solutions have imposed, have led insect development along two apparently divergent paths, each immaculately controlled by a series of chemical messengers or hormones.

The Egg. The eggs of insects occur in a variety of forms, round, conical, sausage-shaped, sometimes with one or more projections or horns. In the unusual case of the parasite *Encyrtus* (Hymenoptera), the egg consists of two bladders connected by a tube; during oviposition, the contents collect in one of the bladders and the other is discarded. It is suggested that having the egg in two packages facilitates its passage through a small hole into the host.

The shell or chorion provided by the mother is often beautifully sculptured and usually contains extensive airspaces. It is made from tanned protein and is not very waterproof but the embryo rectifies this omission by secreting a thin layer of waterproofing wax on the inside of the shell. Since the chorion is laid down in the ovary, some provision must be made to allow for the subsequent entry of sperm. Thus there are one or more tiny funnel-shaped canals called micropyles which pass right through the chorion. In some insects, like the locusts, the chorion is thin and very fragile and the embryo, at an early stage in its development produces a much tougher serosal cuticle on the inside.

In being covered by various impermeable layers, the embryo, just like the adult insect, encounters the problem of obtaining an oxygen supply. Some diffusion of gases does take place through the solid chorion, but in most insects the numerous airspaces inside the chorion are connected together and to the outside air by very small holes. Sometimes these holes are at the tips of 'respiratory horns' especially in eggs such as those on the fruit-fly *Drosophila* which are laid in damp places. Eggs laid in soil can often survive flooding because the air in the chorion acts as a plastron, extracting oxygen from the surrounding water. Eggs which are laid in water, such as those of dragonflies, obtain oxygen from the water. The eggs of many species, both terrestrial and aquatic, absorb water from the environment in the course of development. In some species water is absorbed over the whole egg but often there is a structure specialized for this purpose. The glasshouse White-fly *Trialeurodes vaporariorum* lays her eggs on tomato leaves and each egg has a little horn which is inserted into the leaf tissue and is specialized for the absorption of water. If the leaf wilts, development of the embryo is temporarily arrested. Eggs, like those of Heteroptera and Lepidoptera, which are laid in dry, exposed situations, develop without the uptake of extra water but in many species this is essential for development. The eggs of *Locustana pardalina*, the South African Locust, have been kept in a dried state for three and a half years and, when allowed to absorb water, they completed their development.

Embryo to Larva. After fertilization, the nucleus of the egg cell divides and the daughter nuclei make their way to the surface of the egg to form a layer of cells surrounding the yolk. Part of this layer becomes thickened to form a band of cells from which the embryo develops. Sheets of tissue grow out to make a sac around the embryo and this fills with a fluid called amniotic fluid. The embryo itself grows in such a way as to enclose the dwindling supply of yolk within its body wall. The outer layer of the embryo forms the body wall, the foregut and hindgut, the tracheal and nervous systems and the sense organs. The inner layers form the midgut, the muscles and the circulatory and reproductive systems. These processes, achieved by cell division, differentiation and migration, are controlled by chemical messengers originating at first from centres exerting their effects on the whole embryo. As body segments form, segmental control centres appear and some structures have the effect of inducing development in others.

When the larva is fully developed, it escapes from the egg by rupturing the membranes around it, that is, the serosal cuticle and the chorion. Sometimes an external stimulus acts as the trigger to initiate emergence; in the Human warble fly *Dermatobia* the warmth of the host is the stimulus.

The life-history of a blowfly. Top left: An adult female blowfly, attracted by the odour, seeks out dead or decaying flesh upon which to lay her eggs. Top right: Blowfly larvae. Bottom left: Blowfly pupae. Bottom right: Adult blowflies.

In boring its way out of the egg, the larva first swallows the amniotic fluid, so increasing its body volume. Sometimes this is further increased by the swallowing of air which diffuses in through the shell or enters more rapidly after the initial rupture of the shell. This splitting of the shell is achieved by pumping blood forwards with contractions of the abdomen so that the head presses against the shell. The shell may split irregularly at the area where pressure is exerted but in the blowfly *Calliphora*, and others, there is a special line of weakness along which splitting occurs. In the stick insects (Phasmida) there is a neat, circular cap at one end of the egg which is easily pushed off from inside.

It is not always so easy, however. In the acridids (locusts) and probably also the Heteroptera, the serosal cuticle is too thick and tough to be split in this way. In the locusts the majority of this cuticle is digested away from the inside by the larva before it attempts to emerge. The source of the enzymes which effect this digestion is unlikely in the extreme. The first abdominal segment of many insect embryos bears a pair of knobs believed to be the vestigial remains of ancestral abdominal limbs. It is these structures, the pleuropodia, which in locusts have become glandular and produce the digestive enzymes. If the egg is ligatured around the middle the pleuropodia are sometimes included in the front

101

The life history of the Desert locust *Schistocerca gregaria*. Top left: Mating; centre left: the female lays her eggs underground; bottom left: the egg pod and eggs. Top right: a wingless nymph; bottom right: the adult emerging from the nymph cuticle; the adult fully emerged; and the adult spreading its wings to dry.

half, sometimes the rear and it is only that part of the egg with which the pleuropodia have been included that gets its serosal cuticle digested.

A different aid to emergence is the occurrence, usually on the head, of cuticular spines or hooks known as egg bursters. In the mosquitoes and the tsetse fly *Glossina*, the triangular tooth is set in a membranous hollow in the head cuticle and is erected by blood pressure. The tooth serves to concentrate all the pressure exerted by the larva onto one point on the inside of the egg. Fleas have a similar tooth and when the first hole is made, the larva wriggles along using the egg tooth like a tin opener to cut a slit in the shell. The fruit-fly *Dacus* uses its mouth hooks in a similar way and larvae of Lepidoptera use their mandibles to gnaw their way

through the chorion. After hatching, the larvae continue to eat the shell and in the Cabbage white butterfly *Pieris brassicae*, where a group of eggs are laid together, a newly hatched larva may eat the tops off adjacent unhatched eggs.

The emerged larva proceeds to feed and grow until its inexpansible cuticle will allow of no further growth, at which point the process of moulting occurs.

Moulting. It is popularly believed, quite wrongly, that insects grow only during the brief periods when they are actually shedding their cuticles. In fact, growth in terms of increase in body material is continuous. In soft-bodied larvae the outer layer of the cuticle is wrinkled when first laid down and it stretches and becomes smooth as the insect grows.

More protein and chitin are added to the inner layer of cuticle so that it keeps pace, and it is only when the cuticle is stretched and smooth that it is exchanged for a new one.

In other larvae, like those of the locust, where much of the body is covered with hard, tanned cuticle, this continuous expansion cannot take place. However, the tracheal system is provided with numerous air-sacs and when the cuticle is soft, these are expanded to the full and may occupy almost half the body volume. During growth the air-sacs are reduced in size and the space filled with new body tissue. Even in these hard larvae, some expansion of the cuticle occurs in the joints between the segments of the abdomen. Thus immediately prior to a moult the abdomen is long and distended.

The process of moulting is complex and involves a number of stages. It is initiated by cells in the brain called neurosecretory cells. The axons of these cells end in an organ behind the brain called the corpus cardiacum. From here a brain hormone is released into the blood. This acts on glands in the thorax, the thoracic glands, causing them to release into the blood a moulting hormone. Under the action of this hormone the epidermal cells detach themselves from the old cuticle, grow by cell division and begin to secrete a new soft cuticle. Since it is still contained within the old cuticle, the epidermis can grow only by becoming folded, so the new cuticle is folded too.

When the new cuticle is almost ready, enzymes are poured into the liquid between the old and new cuticles. This moulting fluid can now digest the unhardened inner regions of the old cuticle so that only the hardened outer layer and the waterproofing epicuticle remain. The digested cuticle is absorbed with the moulting fluid through the new cuticle which is itself protected from digestion by a resistant outer covering.

In a soft-bodied caterpillar about 90% of the old cuticle is resorbed and the remaining thin skin is easily cast off. In other larvae, the hard sclerotin of the cuticle over the head and thorax remains but this has a preformed line of weakness along which it splits. On this line, which runs along the top of the head and thorax, there is no sclerotin so that when the softer cuticle is digested away, only the very thin epicuticle remains.

The insect is now ready to emerge and this it does by swallowing air to increase its volume, then contracting specially developed abdominal muscles to increase its blood pressure. The cuticle splits and the insect eases itself out, leaving behind not only its outer covering but also the lining of its foregut and hindgut and the lining of much of the tracheal system. No wonder it comes out gently!

Immediately on emergence, the insect swallows air vigorously so that the still soft cuticle expands. The new cuticle unfolds and stretches and continued

Adult dragonflies lay eggs in or near water. The aquatic larva casts its skin 8–15 times before completing development. At the end of the last stage the adult organs begin to form inside the larval skin. The first of these six pictures of the male *Aeshna*

muscular pumping of the abdomen maintains the blood pressure which distends the head and limbs, and the wings if the emerging insect is an adult. During this expansion, the insect holds on to the substrate with its claws which were specially hardened before moulting started. When expansion is complete, hardening and darkening of the whitish cuticle is brought about by the release of another hormone which promotes the action of the enzymes involved in tanning the cuticle. Hardening and darkening are more or less complete within an hour but hardening continues slowly as more cuticle is added to the inner layers. The onset of hardening cannot be delayed indefinitely so that if only part of the body is incompletely or incorrectly expanded then it 'sets' and remains so deformed.

Growth and Metamorphosis. The growth of insects is, then, punctuated by moults. Between successive moults the insect is known as an instar and the number of instars varies in different species, the majority having between 2 and 20. The immature insects differ from adults in lacking functional wings and sexual maturity. Growth results from an increase in the number, and often the size, of individual cells. The increase in weight resulting from growth is usually considerable. The fully grown larva of the Carpenter moth *Cossus cossus* weighs 72,000 times its original weight and in most insects the increase is at least 1,000 times.

As a rule there is no great difference in body form between larval instars but the change from last instar larva to adult may be very marked. This change is called metamorphosis and insects are commonly grouped in three categories according to the extent of the change at metamorphosis. Ametabolous insects have no metamorphosis. This is typical of the Apterygota; the first instar larvae look like small adults but lack sex organs. At each moult the larvae grow bigger and the sex organs gradually develop. Larvae and adults live in the same habitat and eat the same food.

The Pterygota, on the other hand, can be divided into two groups according to the degree of change at metamorphosis: the hemimetabola and holometabola. In the hemimetabolous insects (for example the locust), the young are miniature versions of the adults except in their lack of wings and functional sex organs. In the larval instars, the developing wings appear externally as wing pads; these orders of insects are consequently alternatively known as exopterygotes. The immature instars of this group of insects are sometimes called nymphs to distinguish them from the caterpillar-like larvae of the holometabolous orders (for example butterflies). In these, the more advanced orders of insect, the larvae are clearly very different in bodily form from the adults and often live in different habitats and eat different food. In these larvae the developing wing buds are

cyanea shows this stage, the nymph in water. It then climbs out of the water, hatches and the adult dragonfly wriggles free of the nymph skin, then hangs clinging to it while its wings expand, harden and dry. Only then is it ready to take wing.

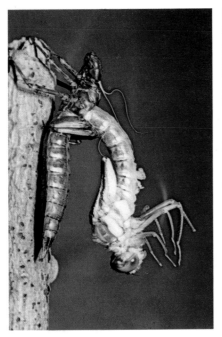

A butterfly emerging from its pupal case. The case has split along a predetermined line of weakness to release the head and legs. Some parts of the new insect's body are already hardened to allow it to move but the wings are soft and must soon be expanded before hardening occurs.

A male mosquito *Culex pipiens* just emerged from the pupa at the surface of the water. After emergence there is a resting period of several hours while the wings expand and harden and flight becomes possible. After this the mosquitoes disperse.

106

Life history of a moth *Actias selene*. Top left: the larva, which becomes inactive and spins a cocoon, top centre. Inside this, the larva changes to a pupa, top right. The adult moth, bottom left, breaks out and waits for its wings to extend before being able to fly, bottom right.

internal, hence the alternative name endopterygotes applied to this group. Most of the reorganization needed to transform the larva into the adult is compressed into a single instar interposed between the last larval instar and the adult. This instar is the pupa.

The Pupa. At the larva/pupa moult, wings and other adult features which have been developing internally are everted and become visible for the first time. Sometimes the wings, limbs and other appendages remain free but usually they fit closely together on the surface of the body and are covered over with a cement so that the whole pupa is fairly immobile.

The pupae of some insects, however, are quite active and utilize behavioural responses as a protective mechanism. The aquatic pupae of mosquitoes rest at the water surface but have special paddles at the end of the abdomen which they use

with great vigour to dive on being disturbed. Since the pupae of most insects are immobile they are rather vulnerable and the majority of insects pupate in a cell or cocoon which gives some protection. Some lepidopterous larvae use a sticky secretion to cement soil particles together to form an underground cell in which to pupate. Other larvae produce silk which may be used to sew leaves together to form a protective chamber for the pupa or, alternatively, the silk is spun into a cocoon surrounding the pupa. In some flies, the last larval skin is not shed but becomes thickened and hardened to form a protective structure known as the puparium. The pupae of many common butterflies are suspended from a silk pad and are quite unprotected apart from adopting the same colouration as their surroundings.

Much speculation has centred on the evolution and significance of the pupal stage. The profound

107

Honeybee pupae, each in its separate cell in the comb. After five days of feeding, the larvae change into pupae and the worker bees cover the tops of the cells with a cap of wax. The limbs and antennae of these pupae are free from the body but little movement takes place.

differences in form and feeding between holometabolous larvae and adults has enabled the same insect to exploit two totally different habitats and lifestyles in the same generation. The different body form between the two stages has, however, necessitated much dismantling and reconstruction during the change-over. It is generally agreed that the developing wing buds inside the thorax do not leave room for the development of wing muscles as well, so that two moults are needed at the end of larval life; one to evert the wing buds and the second to make them functional after the appropriate muscles have been developed. Further, the mode of locomotion is totally different in larva and adult and involves different muscles, so a period of quiescence is obligatory while the old power unit is dismantled and a new one fitted.

Chemical Messengers and Diapause. We have seen how the processes of moulting and subsequent hardening of the cuticle are initiated by chemical messengers or hormones, released by one organ and having their effect on another to which they are conveyed in the blood. Hormones are produced either by special neurosecretory cells in the brain or by other specialized glands. Thus the brain hormone stimulates the thoracic gland to produce moulting

hormone. If at the same time another gland called the corpus allatum, which lies near the brain, produces its hormone, known as juvenile hormone, then the new cuticle produced is typical of a larva. If, however, when the moult is imminent, the corpus allatum produces no juvenile hormone, the cuticle formed is characteristic of an adult. Thus the interplay of hormones controls the development of the insect. Other hormones act to regulate such things as colour changes, egg production and daily cycles of activity.

A major function of insect hormones is the control of growth and development, and if their production is interrupted the insect enters a period of delayed development or diapause. This arrested development can occur at any stage in the life cycle from egg to adult but usually occurs only once and the stage at which it occurs is typical of the species. When it occurs in the adult it results in a delay in the development of the sex organs. This type of dormancy is an adaptation which enables the insect to survive regularly occurring adverse conditions such as winter. In temperate regions, where day length is an indicator of the season, diapause is commonly induced by exposure to shortening days. Often the environmental signal which initiates diapause is received by an earlier stage in the life cycle than that in which diapause actually occurs. This enables the insect to build up its food reserves and become dormant before the weather conditions deteriorate too much.

During diapause the rate of metabolism is very much reduced so that the insect 'ticks over' slowly during the bad times. Certain biochemical changes which occur only at low temperatures are thought to lead to the reactivation of the hormone system so that, subsequently, normal life can be resumed when

Caterpillars of some butterflies spin a pad of silk from glands in the mouth and attach themselves to this by the rear end. Now, the caterpillar spins a loop or girdle of silk to support the front end of its body and, thus secure, changes into a chrysalis.

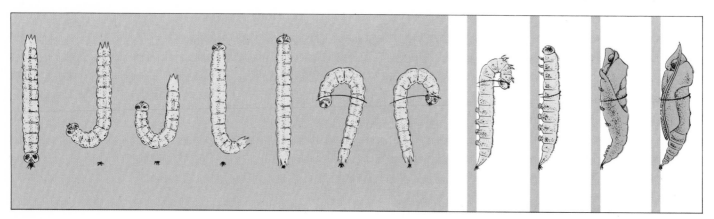

Aphids showing adult and immature forms. In aphids, the young are miniature versions of the adults and no great bodily change, or metamorphosis, is needed to make the transition. Under some conditions the adults are winged but in others they are wingless.

adverse conditions have disappeared and food is again available.

Another range of chemical messengers called pheromones are important in the lives of many insects. Whereas hormones are concerned with regulation within the insect, pheromones are concerned with the co-ordination of individual insects within a population. They are produced by various glands, often on the abdomen, and they most commonly function as sexual attractants. They are generally fairly specific and enable one sex to detect and locate the other often from considerable distances as we shall see later. Sometimes high concentrations of a sex pheromone induce copulation but in other cases a special aphrodisiac pheromone is produced, usually by the male. In social insects, such as termites, pheromones are particularly important in communication between individuals and maintenance of colony structure, as we shall see in the next chapter.

109

Social Insects

Most insects, in common with most other animals, live solitary lives, associating with others of their species perhaps only once in a lifetime in the transient union required for reproduction. Consider, on the other hand, the colony of the honey-bee whose sixty or eighty thousand members, the progeny of the single queen, contribute by their apparently altruistic behaviour to a society whose sophistication and complexity have been a source of wonder since ancient times. Between these extremes lies such a fascinating and extensive range of intermediate behaviour that to draw the line between social and non-social insects is almost impossible.

The 'true' social insects have three characteristics in common; there is some degree of parental care, adults co-operating in caring for the young; there is division of labour, which may or may not involve separate castes devoted to different duties; there is overlap of generations, involving lengthening of the life of some adults – at least the colony mother – so that offspring assist parents for at least part of their

A Wood ant guard on the alert. Division of labour in social insects is nearly always accompanied by the occurrence of physically distinct groups or castes each performing different tasks in the community. This Wood ant is a sterile female.

life. Thus defined, social insects include ants, all termites and some of the bees and wasps.

Presocial Organization. Since these three characteristics can occur independently of each other, we can recognize various levels of presocial organization. In many families of Hemiptera there are species in which parental care occurs, usually of the younger developmental stages and usually by the adult female. For example, in *Gargaphia solani*, which occurs in Virginia, the female guides her brood of a hundred or more nymphs in their migrations from leaf to leaf. She urges them in the right direction and uses her long antennae to keep them together and round up any deserters. In other hemipterans, when danger threatens, the female collects the young under her and covers them with her sturdy body much as a hen will cover her chicks. Even more advanced parental care occurs in the cricket, *Anurogryllus muticus*, of the southeastern United States. The mated female constructs a long underground burrow in which her eggs are laid and protected, by her aggressive behaviour, against all-comers. When the nymphs hatch, they remain near their mother who continues to guard them, manipulating them gently from time to time with her mouthparts. Periodically she lays miniature eggs which the nymphs immediately seize upon and eat. These eggs never hatch and are evidently specialized to act as baby food. The female also keeps the communal burrow wholesome by removing faecal pellets from it. It should be realized that this apparently advanced social behaviour is composed from relatively simple elements commonly used by non-social crickets in the construction of their burrows. The more advanced behaviour requires only the ability to discriminate between the objects manipulated – soil particles, food, faeces and offspring – and slight changes in the behavioural responses to each.

A rudimentary division of labour sometimes arises in aggregations of insects in which differing physical or behavioural abilities result in some individuals performing tasks to the ultimate benefit of other members of the group. The caterpillar-like larvae of the Jack-pine sawfly feed in groups on the tough pine needles of the host plant. They have great difficulty in penetrating the tough cuticle but when one individual, by luck, strength or skill, succeeds in reaching the soft inner tissues, the smell of salivary secretions and plant juices attracts others and soon all the members of the group are able to feed. Conversely, the eggs of the Australian sawfly *Perga affinis* are laid in groups, or pods, inside the leaf tissue. When they hatch, the larvae must break out of the leaf tissue to escape and survive. Usually only one or two individuals are capable of penetrating the leaf and the remainder escape through the holes made by a few. The larger the pod the greater the chance of one of its members being successful. Thus, in a study, it was discovered that the mortality in pods with fewer than 10 eggs was 66 % whilst in pods with more than 30 eggs it was only 43 %.

The occurrence of these elements of social behaviour in isolation may be dead-end specialization or may be stages in the development of true social chance of one of its members being successful. Thus, lent to a fossil record of social behaviour, so stages in its development can only be guessed at, but it is likely that it has developed in different ways at different times. No present-day group of insects represents an evolutionary chain of development of social behaviour, but the living species of wasps give us a clue to the sort of steps which may have led from solitary life to advanced social organization.

Development of Social Organization. Nest building occurs in all true social wasps belonging to the superfamily Vespoidea, but other, non-social, wasps of the superfamilies Pompiloidea and Sphecoidea also build nests. The simplest nest form is the burrow, such as that constructed by the pompilids or spider-hunting wasps. The female wasp catches a spider and paralyses it by stinging. She digs a hole in the ground, puts the spider in, lays an egg on it and stops up the hole with soil, leaving it, never to return. When the wasp larva hatches, it feeds on the spider, kept fresh in its state of paralysis.

An advance on this behavioural pattern occurs in species of the genus *Sphex*, in which a choice of nest site is made before the prey is caught. When the next egg matures in the ovary of the female, she makes another burrow before catching and paralysing a caterpillar to act as food for her offspring. The pompilid *Pseudagenia* also makes her burrow before catching the prey. Particles of mud are dug out, moistened with saliva and used to build a wall around the entrance to the burrow. The wall may serve as a landmark to help the wasp find her nest. It is no great step from this to making a mud nest

A Wood ant worker carrying a cocoon. Cocoons containing pupae are moved around in the nest as conditions change or danger threatens so that they are maintained in optimum conditions as long as possible. The 'ant eggs' sold as fish food are cocoons and not the true eggs.

without a burrow. The potter wasp *Eumenes* collects mud from damp ground and carries it to the nest site, which is often a twig of heather or similar vegetation. Here she daubs the mud on the twig and fashions it into a thin-walled flask, in which she suspends an egg from the roof. The nest is then stocked with several paralysed caterpillars and sealed. Subsequent nests are often built near the first. This is economical when a good nest site has been found and the continuing presence of the female may discourage potential predators or parasites. In all the cases so far described, the egg has been stoppered up with enough food to last the whole larval lifetime – a process known as mass provisioning. The behaviour of another wasp, *Synagris*, is similar to that of *Eumenes* but, if caterpillars are scarce, the larva may hatch before the female has fully stocked the nest, in which case the female goes on bringing food to the feeding larva. This is known as progressive provisioning and occurs in all remaining wasps to be described. Another sphecid, *Ammophila pubescens*, is capable of tending more than one nest if caterpillars are plentiful. In these wasps, the rate of development of eggs in the ovary is more rapid and a second and third egg may be laid before the larva from the first is fully developed. Each morning, the female opens up her three nests and, if there is enough food inside, she closes them again: otherwise she catches more caterpillars to stock them up. In the vespid *Stenogaster*, the female makes a nest of up to 30 cells in a group on the side of a tree. The nest is constructed from particles of sand and mud mixed with rotten wood. The larvae are provisioned progressively and, when fully grown, each seals off its cell with a cap of silk before pupation so that the cell becomes a cocoon. The female may re-use vacated cells and, commonly, the offspring co-exist on the nest site with the original female for some time. *Belanogaster* produces a comb of cells from 'paper', that is, rotten wood chewed up, to make it pliable, and stuck with saliva. The comb, consisting of 50–60 cells, is naked and suspended by a paper stalk from forest vegetation. As the offspring co-exist with the original female and help with all the nest duties, including egg-laying, the colony grows in size, slowly at first and then more rapidly. In favourable conditions, a colony can expand to over 20 adults occupying a nest with up to 200 cells. All the female offspring are fertile but there is some division of labour; the youngest do nest duties, the oldest lay eggs and the others forage. However, there is no evident caste system among the females; they are all the same size and all have well developed ovaries. A rather more elaborate nest is built by the vespid *Polybia*, consisting of several horizontal combs of cells suspended one above the other and covered with a bag-like envelope. Most *Polybia*

colonies are perennial; nests of *P. scutellaris* in Brazil grow to 3 ft (1 m) in diameter and survive up to 25 years. In this genus there are always several queens in each nest, all apparently capable of laying eggs and distinguishable from workers by their greater ovarian development and smaller size. In the nest of *Polistes*, however, there is one dominant queen who may be assisted by a few ancillary queens in founding the nest. The subordination of the ancillary queens is expressed behaviourally; they forage for food and regurgitate it for the dominant queen; they adopt submissive postures to her; they are prevented from egg-laying by her harassment. Any eggs which they do manage to sneak into unguarded cells are likely to be eaten by the dominant queen. During the summer months, the eggs laid by the dominant queen give rise to workers, that is, females with undeveloped ovaries and smaller wings than the queens. The bulk of the adult population of the nest consists of this distinct worker caste which forage for nectar, insect prey and wood pulp for nest-building, thus catering for the needs of the brood, and the queen. In late summer the rate of worker production declines and instead males and fertile females emerge. These reproductive forms gradually replace the short-lived workers during autumn with consequent decline in the welfare of the colony, for these reproductives do no work. Finally the reproductives leave the doomed colony and mate, after which the males die and the females hibernate singly, to await the coming of spring when the colony life cycle starts again. In tropical species, which experience less marked seasonal changes in climate, colonies may persist for several years.

The highest development of social behaviour in wasps thus occurs in the Vespoidea, to which the common wasp, *Vespula*, also belongs. The succession of wasps described here, with ways of life increasing in complexity, is not an evolutionary sequence but one which illustrates one of the possible ways in which social life in insects may have developed.

The Caste System. The occurrence of division of labour in the social insects is nearly always accompanied by the occurrence of physically distinct groups or castes, each performing different tasks in the community. Just as the tasks of egg-laying, foraging and defence are part of the basic behavioural repertoire of all insects, so the bodily forms of the individuals which specialize in particular tasks result from the enhanced development of particular physical attributes. This uneven growth, or allometry, may result in bizarre forms, particularly in soldier castes which sometimes have grotesquely developed heads and jaws to serve in the defence of the colony.

The terms used to describe the members of the insect society – king, queen, soldiers, workers – are, of course, borrowed from the description of human societies but are none-the-less fairly appropriate. The Hymenoptera – bees, wasps and ants – are holometabolous and their larvae are helpless grubs so that all the tasks of the colony are performed by adults and usually females only. In these matriarchal societies, the queen is usually the sole source of individuals because only she lays eggs, while sterile females form the worker caste and, in some ants, the soldier castes too. Males are tolerated in the colony only at certain times and do no useful work. Termites differ not only in having a king as well as a

A termitarium, housing a termite colony, rising like some bizarre ruin of a building. Many species of termites build these mounds, up to 5 m high, which are a feature of tropical landscapes away from jungle or rain-forest.

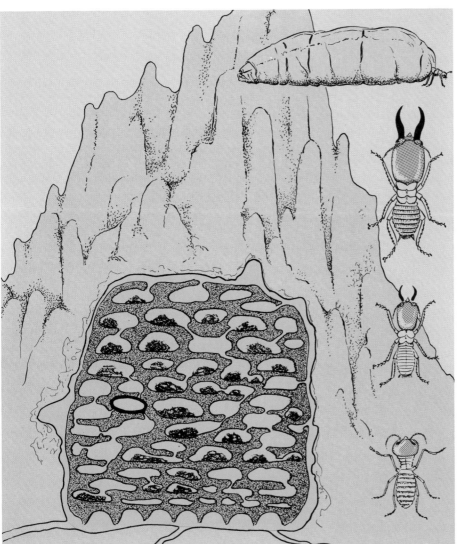

Diagram of a 'termite hill' built from soil and saliva by the co-operative labours of its thousands of inhabitants. The many chambers are interconnected and tunnels run off in all directions from the base of the nest. The insects show, from the top, a queen, a major soldier, a minor soldier, a worker.

113

Termites in Nigeria swarming around a lamp at night. Few of these winged adults are flying much above ground level. After mating and dispersal flights the wings are shed.

queen but, being hemimetabalous, their young differ little from the adults and are in fact the basis of the worker caste. The termite colony may thus be said to be founded on child labour! These juveniles are capable of developing into soldiers or of becoming sexually mature. The castes present in most termite societies are the primary reproductives (king and queen), replacement reproductives (wingless but sexually mature individuals developed from juveniles in the absence of primary reproductives), soldiers of various types and the juvenile workers. There is a series of developmental stages called instars leading to each caste and it is not always easy to distinguish between workers and developmental forms. In the Dry-wood termite *Kalotermes flavicollis* there is a series of larval stages (without wing-pads) leading to several nymphal stages (with wing-pads), all of which act as workers to an increasing extent throughout development. In this species, the sixth larval instar is called a pseudergate or false worker and individuals at this stage can undergo a succession of moults without progressing any further. Additional to these stationary moults, the nymphal stages can undergo regressive moults back to the pseudergate stage. The course of development at these moults is thought to be controlled by the insect's endocrine glands, particularly the corpora allata which produce juvenile hormone. However, the numbers of individuals of each caste within the colony are also closely controlled and depend on the needs of the colony. Thus if replacement reproductives are formed when the king and

queen are still in the colony, the replacements are attacked and destroyed by the workers. Similarly if more soldiers are required, more pseudergates develop into soldiers; but if there are too many soldiers, an appropriate number are killed and eaten by the pseudergates. It follows, therefore, that some overall control is exercised which affects the endocrine system of each individual so that its development and behaviour are appropriate to the needs of the colony. Much of the mystery of this control has been solved by the research of Martin Lüscher who, working with colonies of *Kalotermes flavicollis* over a period of nearly 20 years, has conducted a series of experiments of remarkable ingenuity. Lüscher divided a colony with a wire gauze screen, leaving one half with the king and queen and the other half 'orphaned'. In the orphaned group, several pseudergates developed into replacement reproductives but were soon attacked and eaten by their nest-mates. When a colony was divided by a double wire gauze barrier which allowed no contact between insects on opposite sides, the replacement reproductives which formed in the orphaned side were not this time attacked. The conclusion from these experiments is that the primary reproductives (king and queen)

Termite life cycle. In the Dry-wood termine *Kolotermes flavicollis* development of the different stages in the life cycle are controlled in the normal way by hormones within the individual. Additionally, control is exercised over the colony by the king and queen by means of pheromones as shown in this diagram.

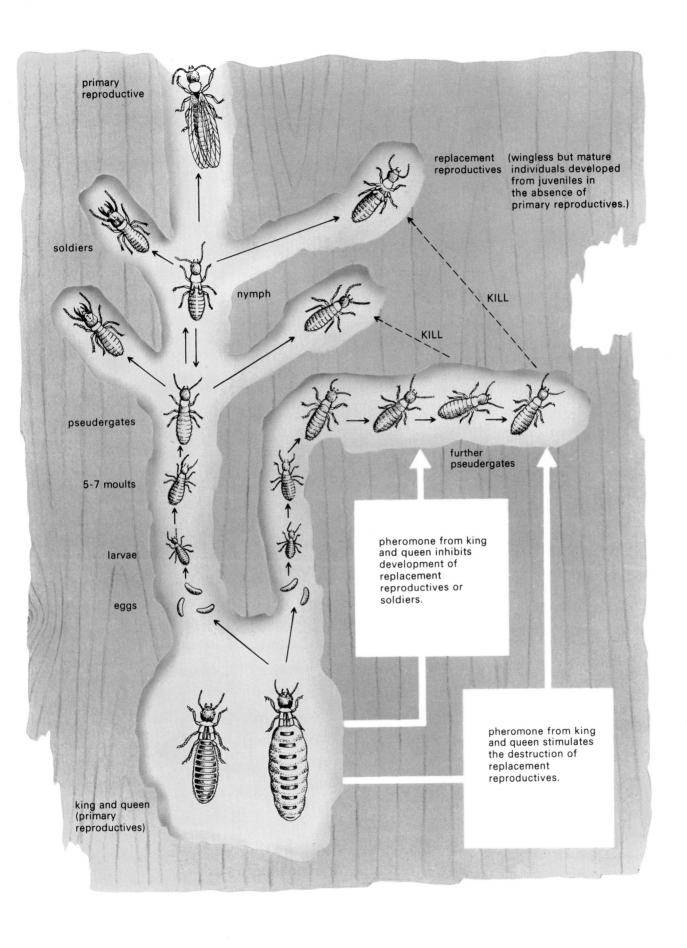

primary
reproductive

soldiers

nymph

replacement
reproductives

(wingless but mature
individuals developed
from juveniles in
the absence of
primary reproductives.)

KILL

KILL

pseudergates

5-7 moults

larvae

eggs

further
pseudergates

pheromone from king
and queen inhibits
development of
replacement
reproductives or
soldiers.

pheromone from king
and queen stimulates
the destruction of
replacement
reproductives.

king and queen
(primary
reproductives)

A soldier termite showing the large and heavily sclerotised head and the powerful jaws. Worker and soldier termites are juvenile individuals of either sex whose development has been arrested at an early stage.

produce a substance which inhibits development of pseudergates into replacement reproductives and that transmission of this inhibition is blocked by the single gauze. Further, the primaries produce a substance by which other members of the colony recognize their presence and will not tolerate the presence of replacements. Transmission of this second substance is blocked by the double screen but not by the single screen through which insects could touch each other with their antennae. Lüscher next fastened primary reproductives in the single screen so that half of the colony was in contact with their head ends and half with their rear ends. This time replacements developed in the half with the head ends, suggesting that the inhibitor was dispersed by the rear end. He found that this continued to be effective if the abdomen was varnished over but not if the

anus was blocked. The mutual feeding or trophallaxis, commonly occurring in social insects, extends in the termites to feeding on the faeces and it is thus that the king and queen dispense their inhibitors. It seemed hardly credible, however, that in a large colony, all the individuals could feed on the faeces of the king and queen. In yet another experiment, pseudergates were fixed in the screen so that their rear ends faced the orphaned group. This time no replacements were produced, indicating that the inhibitor is passed through the intestines of the pseudergates who thus act as middle-men in the spread of inhibition throughout the colony. Strangely, male pseudergates in the screen tended to inhibit the formation of female replacement reproductives and vice versa. Thus pseudergates absorb, and are affected by, the inhibitor appropriate to

116

their sex and pass on that appropriate to the opposite sex. Yet another complexity exists in the production by the primary reproductives (or at least by the king) of a substance which stimulates the production of replacement reproductives of the opposite sex. This marvellously sophisticated system of control is summarized in the accompanying diagram which shows how the composition of the colony is regulated by pheromones, that is to say, by substances produced in small quantities by some individuals and transmitted to others.

A similar system obtains in the honey-bee *Apis*, in which the inhibitory pheromone produced by the queen has been identified as a substance with the impressive name trans-9-keto-2-decenoic acid, but an additional factor in caste determination is the type of food on which the larvae are reared. Any egg of female genetic constitution is capable of becoming either a queen or a sterile worker. If the egg is laid in a normal cell of the wax comb, the larva will be fed for its first three days on a highly nutritious secretion

A sealed honey-bee queen cell from the side. New queens are reared in specially enlarged cells which hang vertically downwards from the comb.

of the salivary glands of workers. Thereafter the larva is fed on a less nutritious mixture of honey and pollen and develops into a worker bee. If, however, the queen's inhibitory pheromone is in low concentration, as might happen if she were old or ill, or if the colony had become very large, then the workers construct so-called royal cells which are larger than normal. Larvae developing in those are fed on royal-jelly, as the nutritious food is called, throughout their larval life and consequently develop into queens.

A queen honeybee, in the centre of the picture, is attended by workers. The queen is specialized for egg laying and cannot do the tasks of workers. In her prime she may lay about 1,500 eggs per day, fertilized eggs giving rise to workers or queens, unfertilized giving rise to drones.

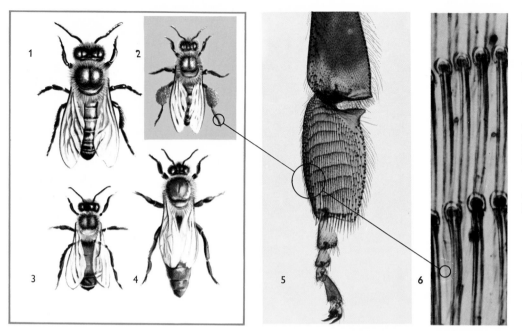

Honeybee castes and the transport of pollen by workers. The bees are (top left) a drone, (bottom left) a worker, (bottom right) a queen and (top right) a worker carrying pollen. The hind leg (centre), enlarged 26 times, shows the 'pollen basket' and (right), enlarged 165 times, the hairs of the basket can be seen.

Thus, either by the influence of pheromones or by virtue of differential feeding, or both, the bodily structure of different individuals varies to produce caste systems. For division of labour to occur it is necessary that different tasks are performed by different individuals. Even within the worker caste, it would be against the best interests of the community if every individual behaved in the same way at the same time.

In many species of ants, workers of two distinct sizes occur and the larger ones are usually called soldiers. The difference in size may be accompanied by differences in form so that soldiers have proportionally larger heads and even larger mandibles than workers. The largest workers of *Anomma nigricans* line their migration routes with forelegs linked and protect their smaller brethren by preventing them from straying from the main body of the ants where they would be set upon by predators. However, the idea that larger workers are soldiers and defend the colony is not true for most ants. The soldiers of many species are less aggressive than their smaller sisters and more inclined to run and hide if the colony is attacked and many large-headed soldiers defend the colony by stuffing their heads into the entrance holes rather than by fighting. By contrast, when the nest wall of the termite *Nasutitermes* is broken open, the defenceless workers and nymphs rush inwards to the depths of the nest but the soldiers mill aggressively on the surface of the nest. In any event, the different bodily forms are associated with different behavioural repertoires.

Differing behavioural responses within the same caste occur in worker honey-bees. The young adult worker cleans cells for about three days, then, as her salivary glands develop, she becomes a nurse and feeds the brood until about day 10. By then her salivary glands are less active and, instead, glands in her abdomen produce wax with which she builds

A busy scene at the entrance to an ant's nest. Intruders are vigorously challenged but some insects are welcomed by the ants as they supply them with attractive secretions. The young of these guests may even be reared by the ants themselves though occasionally they eat the ant larvae.

comb for the nest until day 16. After a few days of receiving and storing nectar and pollen she stands guard at the entrance of the hive; and from the third week until the end of her short life she works as a forager.

Control of Behaviour. Thus the behaviour of individuals is controlled by their caste, or by their age within the caste. But if this control were rigid it might act against the best interests of the colony. There are times in the life of a bee colony when there is a need for additional guards, or additional foragers and, when such a need arises, it is fulfilled. Here then is control at yet another level – control of the behaviour of the colony. Lindauer and his colleagues discovered by painstakingly watching individual, marked bees in an observation hive day and night throughout their lives, that while they stick by and large to the schedule already described, they spend much of their time unemployed. During this time, they wander around the hive inspecting the cells, the honey store, the broad areas, doing jobs as

they come to them. Thus the control of the colony results from individual bees informing themselves of what needs to be done – and doing it.

A similar situation is seen in ant colonies where many individuals may be seen standing about, legs close to body and with antennae folded on their heads – 'resting'. When they do work, however, ants are often seen to co-operate in small groups on a task such as dragging prey home to the nest. Is this yet another level of control? Do the ants communicate their intentions and co-operate knowingly? Hardly. A single ant seeks to pull its prey towards its nest. Since a group of ants comes from the same nest, agreement on the direction of pulling might be expected. However, as each ant seizes the prey at a convenient place and turns with the prey so that its body is orientated for a homeward journey, the result is usually deadlock. The stalemate persists until some ants give up and eventually, by chance, movement in the preferred direction occurs and the prey is efficiently carried home.

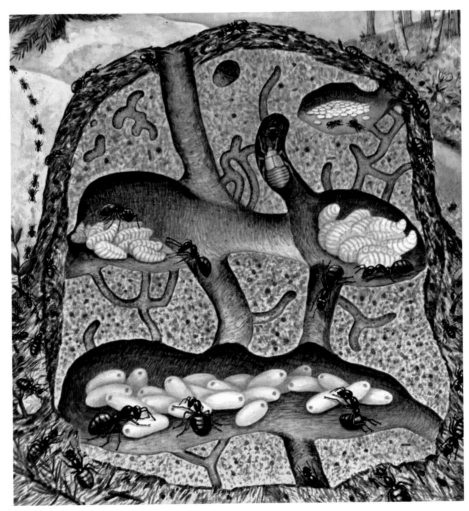

Diagram of a cross-section of a Wood ants' nest showing chambers and interconnecting tunnels with (top right) eggs, (underneath) a guest, (middle left) small larvae, (middle right) big larvae and (bottom) pupae.

119

The nest of a species of Wood ant is constructed from soil and debris and may be more than 3 ft (1 m) high. Colonies of ants live in a great variety of structures usually made by themselves.

Apart from catching the imagination of man through the ages and inspiring some of the most ingenious and elegant scientific investigations, the social insects have had, and continue to have, profound economic effects on mankind. The co-evolution of flowering plants and bees as pollinators has been a major formative influence in the development of plant and animal life on this planet. In most parts of the world ants are among the principle predators of other invertebrates and their biomass and energy consumption exceed those of vertebrates in most terrestrial habitats. Ants are so abundant in the tropics that they replace earthworms as the chief movers of soil and are nearly as important as earthworms in turning the soil in cold temperate forests as well. Termites too, contribute significantly to the turning of the soil and are among the chief decomposers of dead wood and leaf litter in the tropics. One of the most destructive of all insects is the termite *Mastotermes darwiniensis* of northern Australia. Their colonies contain up to a million individuals in each nest. Workers have been seen attacking poles, bridges, trees, crop plants, wool, horn, ivory, vegetables, paper, hay, leather, rubber, sugar, flour, salt, human and animal faeces, billiard balls and the plastic lining of electric cables! Abandoned farms in the outback have been reduced to dust in two or three years – house, fences and all.

Communication and Navigation

Communication between insects involves action on the part of one individual which alters the behaviour of another individual in a predictable way. This rather broad definition encompasses many modes of communication – visual signals, touching, stroking, tapping, grasping, the production of flashes of light, pulses of sound, puffs and squirts of chemical – which evoke responses ranging from simple recognition to the sophisticated co-ordination of activity which we have seen in the social insects. Within the social insects, this repertoire of communicative behaviour may be extended to include elaborate and sometimes bizarre effects such as the exchange of chemical signals conveyed in liquid food which results in the control of caste development and even in programmed execution and cannibalism.

The signals produced by an insect may be of significance to, and may be recognized by, many different species – that is, they are extraspecific. Usually, such signals are concerned with defence and warning, perhaps frightening off an attacker or giving a general warning of the presence of a predator. Conversely, intraspecific signals have significance only for a single species and are largely ignored by members of other species. They are thus commonly used in courtship where they reduce the possibility of interspecific mating and set up

psychological barriers keeping the species apart. As well as identifying the species, the signals used in courtship must indicate the sex of the individual – it would be pointless for a male to attract a male or a female a female – and they must also indicate the position of the individual so that it can be localized and approached. In addition to their use in courtship, intraspecific signals may also be involved in sexual isolation, aggregation, aggression and, in social insects, behaviour such as foraging, recruitment and recognition of nest-mates.

In communication, the information conveyed by the signals is in the form of a code of stimuli using one or more sensory modes which can be produced by the sender and received by the receiver. The most commonly used sensory modes are vision, hearing, smell and taste. For intraspecific signals, since there are many very different species, the sensory mode used should be one which permits a large number of unique signals. It is also important to convey the maximum of information in the minimum of code. Although signal sequences may utilize more than one sensory mode, it is convenient to consider separately visual signals, auditory signals and chemical signals.

Visual Signals. The most visually spectacular of insects are undoubtedly the butterflies with, in many cases, most distinct colour patterns. However, such

Wasps normally kill flies, to feed their larvae, but are predators of other insects, including at times the honeybee. As the wasp struggles with its prey it bites the wings to prevent flight. Here one bee wing is broken, the other already severed.

A queen wasp *Polistes* of North America. In the nest of *Polistes* one dominant queen may be assisted by a few subordinate queens. A dominance hierarchy exists based on the presentation of food by inferiors to superiors.

patterns are not necessarily of signal value. It appears, for example, that the elaborate wing markings of the butterflies of the family Danaidae have little to do with recognition which, instead, depends largely upon scent. In the fruit-fly *Drosophila sub-obscura*, on the other hand, courtship, which involves a series of responses by each sex, depends largely on visual stimuli. The male orientates towards the female and, as they face each other, they both begin to dance, stepping from side to side. When the female stops, the male spreads his wings in a characteristic posture, then circles her and finally

jumps on her, attempting to copulate at the same time.

Some insects have evolved a method of visual communication similar to our own use of morse code transmitted by a pattern of flashing lights. Light production in insects usually has a sexual significance. The male fire-fly *Photinus pyralis* (actually a beetle) exposes light-producing cells on his body and emits flashes of light at intervals of about 5·8 seconds while flying some 20 in (50 cm) above the ground. Females perch on top of low vegetation and if a flashing male comes within about 6 ft 6 in (2 m), the female flashes in response. The female flash is emitted approximately 2 seconds after that of the male and the exact delay between flashes is characteristic of the species. The male approaches any light flash which shows the right time interval, ignoring all others, and as a result of further flashing is led right up to the female. The time relationship between transmission and answer is the all-important characteristic of this signal. Certain species of fire-flies in Burma and Siam form groups which flash synchronously, but the control of this remarkable behaviour is not understood.

A female Glow worm 'calls' to her prospective mate with light signals. Here the female is wingless and resembles the larva. The male is fully winged and has well developed compound eyes.

Many ants of the genus *Formica* are especially adept at detecting moving objects and, while the worker ants often ignore prey insects that are standing still, they run towards the prey as soon as it begins to move. The sight of a running worker is often enough to set other workers running and the chase is joined. In some species, when foraging workers encounter an insect they dash in erratic circles around it and thereby attract other workers in the vicinity. It is thought that the excited, broken running pattern of behaviour in ants which have just discovered prey may be a ritualized form of normal running evolved specially to function in this situation as a visual signal. Alternatively it may be simply incidental to the increased movement necessitated by the chase, but in either event, there is no doubt that the response of the other workers results in the capture of more prey and that this interaction between ants is a form of visual communication.

In the process of foraging, ants may travel considerable distances from their nest, changing direction many times, but they usually have no difficulty in finding the nest again. The idea that ants find their nest after a journey by the sight, smell or sound of it was disproved by so-called displacement experiments. In these experiments foraging ants were picked up and replaced a little way off. Often these ants were unable to find their way home although they could have returned from greater distances on their own journeys. Further investigation showed that ants could use two senses, antennal chemical sense and vision, to find their way to and from their nests. If a worker of *Lasius niger* is set the task of carrying back to its nest a pile of pupae which have been placed in the centre of a large turntable it can find its way even if the turntable is rotated between its outward and homeward trips. It loses its way, however, in the dark. Alternatively, a related species of ant, *L. fuliginosus* is capable of carrying out this task in complete darkness but is lost if the turntable is rotated or its surface cleaned between outward and homeward trips. In this case, the ant is relying on a chemical sense to find its way whereas *L. niger* was orientating to distant visual landmarks. The two methods of navigation are not, of course, mutually exclusive.

Ants using visual navigation usually orientate to distant landmarks, often the sun, which they sense with their eyes. This was strikingly demonstrated by an experiment of Santschi's carried out under natural conditions. An ant running in sunshine was shaded by a small screen and at the same time the sun's light was reflected on to it from the opposite side by a mirror. The ant turned and ran in a new direction so that its body lay at the same angle to the reflected light as it had previously lain to the sun.

These menotaxes, or light-compass reactions, in which the insect's body is maintained at an angle to the light, are a development of the simpler phototaxes in which the insect's body points directly at or away from the light. Inexperienced ants which are just learning to forage use phototaxes, but later they become able to use menotaxes and also, of course, to compensate for the fact that the sun's position alters in the sky by about 15° in each hour. Experienced ants can also follow a crooked course outwards and return by a course which is more or less the shortest straight line. Something about the way the ant makes this calculation is shown by experiments with two lights. During training of the ants, one light was shown for 30 seconds at an angle of 135° to their course. The other light was then shone for 10 seconds at an angle of 225° to their course and this alteration of lights was kept up for the whole training period. When these ants were later tested with a single light that shone all the time they orientated to it on a course of 159°. This is approximately the third side of a triangle which has one side of 225° and another three times as long at 135°. In other words it is the resultant straight line course as can be seen in the diagram.

Auditory Signals. Sounds are produced by many insects in the course of their day-to-day activities and may have little or no significance in the life of the insect. However, many sounds do have significance as signals. These sounds are produced by special mechanisms and are detected by tympanal organs – the equivalent in insects of our ears. In some Orthoptera and Coleoptera, sounds are commonly produced by frictional mechanisms. A ridge is scraped over a series of grooves on another part of the body which is thus caused to vibrate. In some Homoptera and Lepidoptera, on the other hand, a thin membrane is set vibrating by the direct action of special muscles.

Sound signals which are used in intraspecific communication usually consist of discrete bursts of sound separated by intervals of silence and repeated in a regular manner. Such are the songs of insects, and some species have a variety of different songs for different occasions. The songs differ in the timing of sounds and are used most commonly in courtship but some songs also lead to aggregation of particular species and separation of different species.

Most grasshoppers and locusts (Orthoptera) produce sounds by rubbing a ridge on the inside of the hind leg against a knobbly vein on the outside of the folded wing. This friction causes the wing to vibrate at its own resonant frequency which varies from 2–50 thousand cycles per second. Each stroke of the leg produces a single pulse of sound. The sounds can be recorded and produced visually as an oscillogram, as in the diagram, which shows the differences between the songs of the males of four common British grasshoppers. Often female grasshoppers are capable of singing too but do so only when they are sexually mature. The courtship behaviour of the British grasshopper *Chorthippus brunneus* is fairly typical. The male sings his calling song and if a

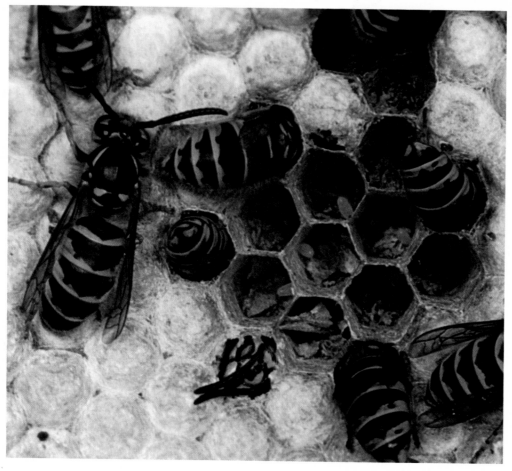

Part of the comb in a nest of the Common European wasp. In the open cells, a small, whitish egg can be seen near the base of each.

Honeybee workers and a larger, stocky drone. The sole function of the drones is to fertilise the queen during the nuptial flight. To this end they have powerful thoracic flight muscles and large eyes.

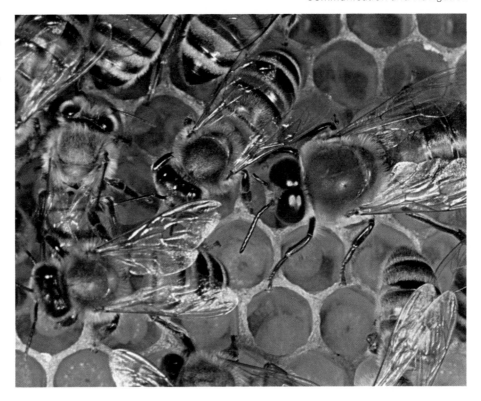

Part of the comb of the Common wasp with well developed larvae in some of the cells. Those cells whose tops are sealed over contain pupae.

125

responsible female hears it she sings a similar song in reply. By pausing to listen to each other's sounds, the two insects are able to orientate to each other and move closer. When the male sees the female he starts to sing his courtship song. If, however, another courting male intervenes, the two rivals sing an aggressive song at each other until one of them gives way and withdraws. Whilst singing the courtship song, the male hops towards the female; eventually he hops onto her and attempts to copulate. If he is rejected he starts the courtship song again. If, during copulation, the female becomes restive or tries to move away, the male sings a copulation song which calms her and allows copulation to progress.

Chorthippus brunneus is very closely related to another grasshopper species, *C. biguttulus*, and the two can be distinguished only with difficulty. They have very similar mating behaviour and crossing occurs readily in the laboratory to produce healthy offspring. Yet although they live in the same habitat, very little crossing occurs in the field. The reason for this relates to the major difference between the species – their songs. The songs of each species stimulate both male and female members of that species to copulate much more effectively than do the songs of the other species. These differing behavioural responses result in effective isolation of the two species.

A different method of sound production by friction is used by crickets (Grylloidea) and long-horned grasshoppers (Tettigonioidea). In these insects the fore wings or elytra are somewhat hardened and parchment-like in consistency and act as shields for the more membranous hind wings. Each elytron has a vein on the underside modified to form a toothed file while on the edge of the opposite elytron there is a ridge which acts as a scraper. In sound production, the elytra are raised above the body at an angle of about 45° and opened and closed like the blades of a pair of scissors. This causes one of the scrapers to rasp along one of the files causing the elytron to vibrate and produce a sound. The sounds thus produced can be very penetrating; the House cricket *Brachytrypes megacephalus* is said to make a noise that can be heard over a distance of 1 mile (1·6 km). However, the sounds are often quite musical and in some parts of the world crickets are sold in cages to be kept as singing pets.

A typical cicada, large plant-sucking insects famous for their shrill and monotonous song. Only the males make the sound but males and females may congregate in response to it.

As before, different songs for different occasions are produced by varying the length of the sound pulses and the intervals between them. The use of aggressive songs is well illustrated by crickets. In *Oecanthus* each male occupies a territory of about 7·75 sq in (50 sq cm) in which he identifies himself by singing his normal song. If another male enters his territory he challenges it with his aggressive song and the intruder replies. If song power is not sufficient to resolve the conflict, fighting may occur. The males lash each other with their long antennae and jostle and bite till one retires defeated. These contests lead to the establishment of a dominance hierarchy and also ensure that males are spread out throughout the habitat, thus increasing the chances of encounters between males and females and making successful mating more likely.

The same effect is achieved in essentially the opposite way by some cicadas (Homoptera). They have a song which leads to aggregation of both males and females so that clumping of a species within the habitat tends to occur. In North America there are three species of *Magicicada* which occur in the same habitat. Crossing between the species occurs readily in laboratory conditions but not under natural conditions. This is due to aggregation of each species in response to their different songs so

that particular trees may be occupied more or less exclusively by a particular species. The effect is increased by the tendency of different species to sing in chorus at different times of the day.

The sound produced by cicadas is rather monotonous and very shrill; in a tropical forest the volume of sound produced can be quite deafening. The sound is produced by the vibrating membranes of a pair of drum-like organs called tymbals which are situated on either side of the first abdominal segment. The thin cuticular membrane of the tymbal is supported by a thick circular rim and various internal compression struts. A powerful muscle is attached to the inside of the tymbal. When the muscle contracts the tymbal buckles inwards like a tin lid, producing a loud click as it does so. On relaxation of the muscle, the elasticity of the cuticle causes the tymbal to buckle out again. The tymbal is backed by air-sacs so that at each inward click it is free to vibrate at its own resonant frequency. By raising the abdomen and stretching the folded membrane, the insect can alter the size of the air-sacs and so tune their resonant frequency to that of the tymbals, thus increasing the volume of sound. The cicad has an organ of hearing adjacent to the tymbal but while it is singing it keeps the hearing organ creased and inoperative, thus avoiding damage to its

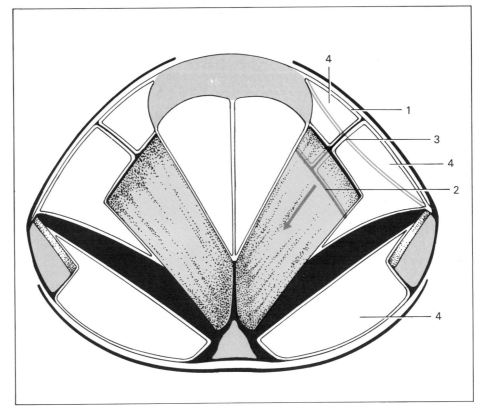

A diagrammatic section through the first abdominal segment of a cicada. Sound is produced by buckling of the tymbal (1), a thin disc of cuticle. The tymbal muscle (2) is connected to the tymbal by a strut (3). Contraction of this muscle (right side of diagram) causes the tymbal to buckle inwards producing a click which is amplified by resonance in the underlying air sacs (4). On relaxation of the muscle, elasticity of the muscle causes the tymbal to buckle out again. On the underside of this abdominal segment, a folded membrane can be stretched to tune the air sacs to the resonant frequency of the tymbal.

127

Workers of the Common European wasp on the outside of their nest constructed from chewed up wood fibres. The typical mature nest has the size and shape of a football. The entrance is at the base, inside are horizontal layers of comb separated by pillars.

auditory system by the high intensity of sound in its own song.

Sounds having only extraspecific significance are not usually organized into regularly repeated pulses and are commonly produced by both males and females. Warning sounds are sometimes accompanied by visual warning displays. When disturbed, the Peacock butterfly opens its wings suddenly to display the large eye spots and at the same time the opening wings produce a hissing noise. The combined effect may scare off a predatory bird. The tiger moths (Arctiidae) are distasteful species and are marked with very bright warning colours which helps predators to learn to avoid them. They also produce sounds by means of tymbals, and sound production is most readily elicited in the less distasteful species, these being the forms which most need to reinforce their display if predators are to learn to associate the display with unpalatability. It is also suggested that the sounds produced by their tymbals can be used to 'jam' the echolocation system of hunting bats. Some insects, harmless in themselves, obtain protection by mimicking distasteful or dangerous species and sound signals may be enlisted in this deception. Many hoverflies not only look like bees but they sound like them too and the burying beetle *Necrophorus*, which looks superficially like a bumble bee, buzzes like one when disturbed.

Chemical Signals. The most remarkable of chemical signals are the pheromones, substances secreted externally which, if passed to another individual of the same species, cause it to respond in a particular way. Since they are concerned with the co-ordination of individuals, they are of importance in sexual behaviour and, as we have seen, in controlling behaviour and physiology in social insects.

A remarkable example of the power of pheromones to elicit a response at a distance and when in very low concentration is found in the sex attractants in butterflies and moths (Lepidoptera). The famous French naturalist Fabre described how in many species of moths, males would assemble round a female or even round an empty box which had contained her. His claim that the males came from miles away, attracted to her scent, was hard to believe when the small amount of chemical a female

128

could produce was considered in relation to the large volume of air into which it would have to be released. Experiments have subsequently shown, however. that Fabre was right. The males come from downwind and the presence of pheromone stimulates upwind flight so that they are guided to the female by the wind and not by a concentration gradient of the very feeble chemical stimulus. Only when they are very near to the female does the concentration of chemical become sufficiently high for the male to follow the concentration gradient. A concentration of pheromone of only 3,250 molecules per cubic inch (200 per cu cm) is adequate to stimulate upwind flight in the male of the moth *Bombyx mori*. The female stores about 10^{14} molecules of the attractive substance called bombycol in her gland reservoirs and this is enough to produce a threshold concentration in a volume of air of elliptical shape, drawn out several miles downwind.

It is well known that individual colonies of ants and bees have their own colony odour shared by all the members, and that intruders, even of the same species, are challenged as enemies by the workers guarding the entrance to the nest. Indeed, members of a colony returning from foraging trips are challenged by their own guards if they have been away for a long time. This suggests that, on an individual away from the nest, the colony odour loses its strength or that the colony odour itself is gradually changing. The latter seems likely in the case of honey-bees where the scent is derived from the incoming food which is shared amongst the colony. Every time the main source of food changes, the colony odour changes too, hence the rough reception accorded to stragglers who have been out while the change took place.

Ants have been shown to use chemicals in navigation as mentioned above. Some ants can be seen moving in files, one behind the other but not necessarily close behind. If the path is cleaned between two ants, the following ant stops when it reaches the cleaned part. Other ants following on the same path also stop and there may be some delay before any cross the cleaned area and continue on the path. Experiments show that ant trails are due to scent deposited on the ground from specialized glands. It is likely that ants use their antennae in detecting the scent and careful observation suggests that the trail exists not on the ground but in the air as a tunnel of scented air, a cross-section of which at

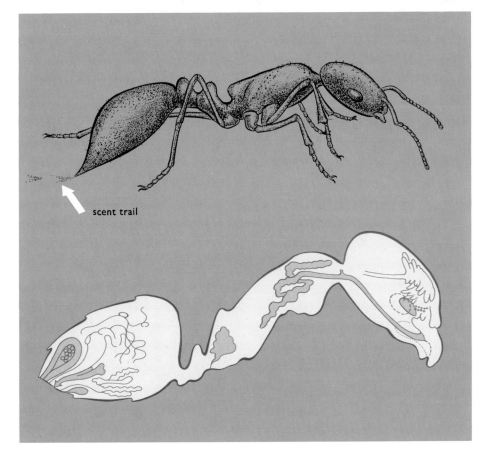

scent trail

An American Fire ant leaves a scent trail which leads other ants to food objects too bulky for one ant to retrieve. The scent markings are arrow-shaped as a result of initial pressure the sting; this enables other ants to recognize the direction of the trail. The lower picture shows the scent glands, each producing a different pheromone, from which a combination of meanings may be expressed.

A side view of a comb in which a cell has been cut open to show a wasp pupa inside. The eye pigment is well developed, but the wings, lying between the second and third legs are small and will be expanded when the adult emerges.

Odours play a large part in the organisation of a honeybee colony. This worker is exposing scent glands on her abdomen and fanning her own scent into the air with her wings.

130

The language of bees: (1) round dance, for distances less than 160 ft (50 m); (2) figure-of-eight dance, for distances over 100 yd (100 m), the actual distance being indicated by the speed with which the abdomen is wagged, the greater the distance the more slowly it is wagged; (3) represents a source of nectar, and (4) the hive, and in the bottom row is shown the pattern of the figure-of-eight dance according to the position of the source of nectar relative to the sun.

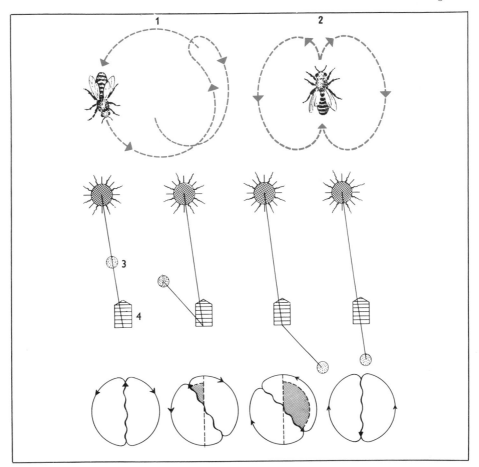

right angles to the ant's path would be a semicircle.

The most sophisticated of communication and navigation occurs in the honey-bee. Consider the control of foraging and other activities, say, in relation to temperature control. Bees maintain the temperature of the brood nest between 94° F (34·5° C) and 96° F (35·5° C) irrespective of outside temperature. To do this they must be able to heat or cool the hive. Heating is accomplished by clustering over the brood area and producing warmth by muscle vibration. Cooling is achieved initially by fanning but, in extremes, water is spread over the combs and its evaporation produces the required cooling. Both heating and cooling require social communication but this is most involved in the evaporation of water. It might be supposed that bees, detecting the overheating, rush out and obtain water to spread in the hive, but this is not so. The spreaders are bees whose normal task is to receive incoming food and they remain in the hive. Of the foragers, only a few will know the whereabouts of water in the terrain and most will be engaged in bringing in nectar and pollen. How then is water obtained without delay, in the right amount and

only for as long as it is needed? Homecoming foragers offer their burdens to receiving bees and go out again only when they have delivered their load. If this takes a long time and they are not received with enthusiasm they are discouraged from collecting any more of that material. In times of heat stress, any forager who happens to return with water will be relieved eagerly, perhaps by three or four bees at once. This stormy begging induces eagerness in the forager and she performs a recruiting dance to stimulate hive bees to fly out to the water source. When the emergency is over the water carriers have to run around the hive trying to find a bee that will relieve them of their load and they become discouraged and are subsequently recruited by nectar or pollen collectors again.

The way in which successful foragers recruit and direct other bees to a food source is one of the most extraordinary examples of communication between insects. When food is located within about 160 ft (50 m) of the hive, the finder performs the so-called round dance on the surface of the comb in the hive. During the circling movements of this dance the bee is followed by other potential foragers attracted by

Right: A small colony of Venezuelan tree wasps on their nest. Some of the cells contain young larvae, others have already been sealed over.

Left: A queen Tree wasp at the entrance to her nest. In this species the comb is concealed within a protective envelope.

the movement. They obtain from the dancing bee chemical clues which identify the food – flower scent on the bee's body and chemicals in the food which she regurgitates to the receivers – and are themselves stimulated to go out and search for it. When the food source is beyond 280 ft (85 m), a 'figure of eight' dance is performed which, in addition to giving chemical clues, informs the followers of the direction and distance of the food. The orientation of the straight part of the dance with respect to the vertical

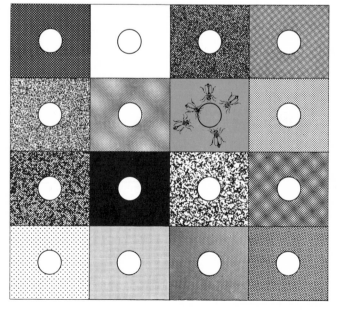

One of the experiments carried out by von Frisch. Bees which had found food regularly in a glass bowl placed on a blue background, immediately fly to a piece of blue paper (without food) in the centre of 15 other pieces of paper, coloured in shades between black and white. The experiment does not succeed with red as bees do not see this as a colour. Bees trained on yellow will also fly to yellow-green and orange-red. Bees often confuse purple and violet with blue but not blue-green.

reflects the orientation of the food from the hive in relation to the position of the sun. If the bee runs directly up the comb in the straight part, the food lies in the direction of the sun, if the straight run is at 45° to the right of vertical, the food is at 45° to the right of the line from the hive to the sun. During the straight run, the bee waggles her abdomen from side to side emitting pulses of sound as she does so. The number of pulses during the straight run is related to the distance from the hive to the food.

The figure of eight dance is also used when bees are searching for a new home. In a flourishing hive, part of the colony may emerge with the old queen as a swarm and establish themselves in a new locality. First they cluster on any suitable object such as a branch of a tree. Then scout bees are sent out to find a permanent home. Each successful scout announces the locality of her favoured site by means of the dance performed on the surface of the cluster of bees. Other bees are recruited by the dancers to inspect the various sites offered and the suitability of each site is reflected in the vigour and enthusiasm with which returning bees dance. Eventually, one of the potential sites gains most favour and the swarm 'agrees' on this before moving off. This process may last for several days, and on one famous occasion Martin Lindauer watched a swarm for four days, noting directions of potential sites indicated by the dances and calculating their distances. Eventually, with the aid of stopwatch and compass, he had the locality of the site which was rapidly gaining favour and, armed with this knowledge, he was able not simply to follow the swarm to its new dwelling but to arrive there before the bees did!

Much of the inter-action between insects, and between insects and other animals, is competitive. The competition is for food, for living space, for survival itself, and the pressures which this competition imposes on individuals are very considerable. The restraining effect of that competition is well illustrated by a calculation once made of the potential reproductive capacity of the small fruit-fly *Drosophila*. Bred in ideal conditions, they may produce 25 generations a year and a female can lay up to 100 eggs, of which about half will become males and half females. If a colony were started with a single pair, and they and their offspring were allowed to breed under ideal conditions for a year, at the end of the 25th generation the colony would contain about 10^{41} flies. If those flies were packed tightly together, 1,000 to a cubic inch, they would form a ball whose diameter would be 96 million miles, almost the distance from the earth to the sun!

The fruit-fly is not alone in having this prodigious capacity for reproduction, but clearly in no case is it ever realized. In addition to lack of food, inclement weather and other physical hazards, the depredations of predators play a significant role in curtailing the number of insects. Those insects which survive to reproduce are most likely to be the ones which are best able to avoid being eaten, and characteristics which contribute to that ability are passed on to successive generations and become firmly established as features of the species. Thus many strange and elaborate defensive mechanisms have been evolved.

One of the simplest methods of avoiding the attentions of predators is to remain hidden. Many insects, particularly the larvae of moths and beetles, derive some protection by living in the soil. Similarly the ant lions (Neuroptera) remain below ground in their ant-capturing pits until emerging as adults. Such insects, however, are never entirely free from predation; even in the apparent security of a tunnel in wood, the larvae of the wood wasp *Sirex* may fall victim to the inch-long ovipositor of the ichneumon, *Rhyssa*. In this case the remarkable ovipositor, capable of boring through wood, has evolved as a weapon to counter the concealing strategy of the potential victim. This sort of 'arms race' typifies the co-evolution of prey species and their predators or parasites. We shall now look in more detail at some of the strategies of potential prey species.

Resembling the Surroundings. The most common method of concealment employed by insects is camouflage. Animals which are camouflaged to resemble part of their surroundings are said to be cryptic or show cryptic colouration. Good examples are the green or brown colour of many grasshoppers or caterpillars. A famous, and much repeated, experiment was carried out about seventy years ago using green and brown varieties of the European mantid *Mantis religiosa* with wild birds as predators. Two groups of mantids, both containing green and brown varieties, were tethered in the open for 18 days; one group was tethered on green vegetation

This leaf insect relies on its remarkably close resemblance to an inedible object, a leaf, to afford it protection against predators. The veins, fungal spots and blemishes are copied in faithful detail. There are only two real leaves in this picture.

Protectively coloured Common marbled carpet moths, *Dystroma truncata*. The broken colour pattern of these moths enable them to merge into the similarly dappled tree trunk on which they rest.

and the other group on brown vegetation. It was found in both cases that all the conspicuous insects had been eaten whilst all those which harmonized in colour with the background survived.

Thus an animal may be cryptic in one habitat but very conspicuous in another and predators are likely to eliminate any animal which settles in the wrong place. Consequently evolutionary pressure has ensured that most insects which rely on crypsis are capable of selecting an appropriate background. In most cases this appears to be an innate response to colour rather than a behavioural response in which the insect compares its own colour to that of the background and selects the best match. The moth *Rhododipsa masoni* rests on the flower heads of *Gaillardia aristata*. The flower has a yellow centre surrounded by a red area and finally by a ring of yellow petals. The head and thorax of the moth are yellow and the wings are red. The vast majority of resting moths sit radially facing either towards or away from the centre of the flower so that the yellow and red areas of both moth and flower overlap. This remarkable matching occurs because only the red parts of the flower have nectar and the moth sits in the best position for feeding from them, which coincides with the best position for camouflage.

If an insect has to blend perfectly with its surroundings there will be relatively few situations in which it can achieve the perfect harmony. One way round this problem is for the insect to change colour to suit the surroundings in which it finds itself. This ability, so well known in the chameleon, is but poorly developed in insects and usually occurs only at moulting. Pupae of butterflies such as *Pieris brassicae*, and various species of *Papilio* can be

either green or brown depending on the immediate surroundings of the caterpillar prior to pupation, but the mechanism is not infallible and 'errors' do occur.

Certain predators, particularly birds, succeed in detecting cryptic prey by learning a so-called searching image. If they are looking for moths, they look for the triangular symmetry of the wings. Some prey species have overcome this by developing disruptive colouration, a technique widely copied in military camouflage. Many cryptic moths have bold disruptive patterns which break the outline of the animal so that parts of it fade separately into the background. Sometimes striped patterns on the moth's wings blend with vertical stripes on the tree trunk on which it rests. Such a moth almost invariably rests in the correct orientation for this to be successful.

Resting moths usually apply themselves closely to the substrate, so reducing the shadow around their margins, which might give them away to a searching predator. It is less easy for cylindrical caterpillars to do this, but in some cases they have developed the technique of counter-shading. The underside of a resting caterpillar is in deeper shadow than the upperside but this is compensated by the natural colouring on the underside being lighter. The caterpillar then looks flat and the tell-tale cylindrical appearance is avoided.

In different parts of the country, the same species of insect may be associated with different backgrounds and most of the population in a given area are coloured accordingly. The underside of the Grayling butterfly *Satyrus semele* is whitish in specimens from chalk districts but more brown in moorland specimens. This is even more marked in

Typical, intermediate and melanic forms of the Peppered moth *Biston betularia* (right centre, top left, bottom left) furnish one of the best known examples of evolution taking place before our eyes.

the case of black forms of various moths which have appeared in industrial areas of Britain and Europe during the last century. A well studied example of this industrial melanism is seen in the Peppered moth *Biston betularia*. The typical form is mottled grey and white and is cryptic when resting on lichen-covered tree trunks. There is another, black, form which contributed to less than 1 % of the population in Britain before 1850. However, with the growth of industry in the North and Midlands, smoke from the factories killed off most of the lichens on trees and replaced them with a sooty deposit. Against this background the black form of the Peppered moth was better camouflaged and increased in numbers in these regions while the typical form declined. By 1895, in the Manchester area, 95 % of moths were of the black form and they still are today.

Resembling Something Inedible. Large numbers of palatable insects are quite conspicuous in their resting places but are not eaten because the predators do not recognize them for what they are. Geometrid caterpillars (Lepidoptera), stick insects (Phasmida), and mantids (Dictyoptera) all resemble twigs and rest amongst twigs similar in diameter to themselves. They commonly sway to and fro imitating the movement of a twig in the wind. Other insects including mantids, phasmids, butterflies and grasshoppers mimic leaves. They often have markings resembling veins and the various blemishes, fungal spots, bird droppings and ragged edges that occur in leaves are copied with remarkable attention to detail. Butterflies such as the Tortoiseshell and Comma rest with wings closed and resemble dead leaves.

Bird droppings are often deposited conspicuously on leaves but are seldom eaten by other birds. Many caterpillars, such as those of the swallowtail butterflies *Papilio* acquire protection by mimicking bird droppings when they are small. At this stage they rest in full view on leaves. But later they become too large to resemble bird droppings and then they become green in colour and change their behaviour pattern to rest cryptically on the undersides of the leaves.

Behaviour on Discovery. Once the deception of mimicry has been discovered and the predator

Top : A swordgrass moth which, even seen close-to, bears a great resemblance to a piece of stick. Centre left : A looper or stick caterpillar of the Brimstone moth *Opisthograptis luteolator*. Centre right : The leaf-like Bush cricket *Tanusia brullati* of South America. Bottom left : The Privet hawk moth *Sphinx ligustri* caterpillar feeding. Bottom right : *Cilix glaucata*, a moth that resembles bird droppings.

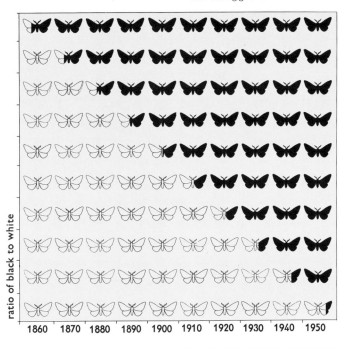

ratio of black to white

1860 1870 1880 1890 1900 1910 1920 1930 1940 1950

Chart showing how the melanic form of the Peppered moth increased in industrial areas from 1% to 99% of the population from 1848 to 1948.

approaches, the insect prey have a variety of responses in their repertoire which may prevent the ultimate disaster. They may seek to exaggerate the original mimicry; the stick insect when disturbed increases its apparent length by stretching its legs out in line with its body. It may also drop off its perch and lie motionless, feigning death. This device is also used by some beetles, bugs and grasshoppers. The response of the predator is often to lose interest and move away.

Bagworm caterpillars (Lepidoptera) live in tubes which they make for themselves from silk. The tubes are camouflaged by pieces of stick and leaves attached to the outside. When disturbed, the caterpillar withdraws hastily into the tube and seals the opening by pinching its margins together. Where no such prepared retreat is available, the prey may resort to flight. Again many devices have evolved to confound the enemy. The cryptically coloured underwing moths display conspicuous red or yellow hind wings when in flight but on alighting the wings are immediately closed, rendering the insect cryptic again. It is believed that the predator, following the bright colour, is baffled by the sudden disappearance of its target.

Alternatively, when discovered by a predator, many insects produce a display which appears to be designed to startle the predator. The male stick

The long hairs on the body of this lepidopteran caterpillar *Acronycta tridena* make it unpalatable for would-be predators. The conspicuous colouration makes it easier for the predators to learn to avoid it.

Eyed hawkmoth *Smerinthus ocellatus* at rest (bottom left) shows only cryptically patterned wings. Alarmed (bottom right), the hind wings are parted revealing a pair of menacing 'eyes', which are sufficient to scare away a bird.

insect *Oncotophasma martini* curls up the swollen tip of its abdomen in a striking imitation of a scorpion. Other stick insects flash open highly coloured wings which are normally concealed. This flash behaviour, employed by many orders of insects, is most effective if the brightly coloured region takes the form of concentric rings, which resemble eyes. It has been shown by experiment that the effectiveness of the eyespots increases with the perfection with which

they mimic true eyes. In some moths this is taken to considerable lengths, but much less impressive eye-spots on the wings of several of our common butterflies appear to have a different function. It seems that the value of these 'eyes' lies in the fact that they are well away from the vital organs of the body and that they invite attack. Thus a Meadow brown may survive having its wings shredded by an attack that would be fatal had it been directed at the head.

A Praying mantis (top) in the normal relaxed attitude will assume a most grotesque posture (bottom) when alarmed, calculated to inhibit a predator's attack.

141

The African mantis *Pseudocreobota ocellata* has a conspicuous eye-spot on each fore wing. When threatened by an enemy, the mantis displays its wings in a way which is disconcerting to humans and may frighten away an enemy.

The Polyphemus moth *Telea polyphemus* of north America is 12.5 cm across the spread wings. It is remarkable for the details of the eye-spots on the hind wings which give it a startling appearance.

142

Fighting Back. Insects are by no means defence-less and many can deter would-be predators by the use of mouthparts, claws and spines on the legs. The spines on the fore legs of mantids have been seen to inflict considerable damage on small lizards which had misjudged their prey.

Additional to this general armoury, many insects are venomous. The poisons of insects probably evolved by chance as by-products of metabolism and, being found useful, have been retained. As well as being defensive weapons, these poisons are used by insects for killing or paralyzing their prey. Apart from this, the blood-sucking insects, like mosquitoes, inject saliva into the wound as they feed. The saliva is not a poison but nevertheless the human body often reacts with swelling and intense itching. The bites of many insects are accompanied by the injection of poison produced in special glands associated with the mouthparts. Similar glands associated with the egg-laying apparatus occur in certain bees, wasps and ants. Here the ovipositor has become modified into a sharp, pointed sting specifically for the injection of venom and eggs are laid without its aid. The venom of these insects produces a very painful reaction and can be dangerous to humans. Many poisonous insects can squirt their poisons, often accurately, some distance at a menacing predator. Others emit fluids or vapours, not actually poisonous but sufficiently unpleasant to ward off an attack.

Another line of chemical defence developed by some insects is the possession of substances in their bodies which render them distasteful to predators. A bird which has eaten such an insect may soon afterwards be so sick that it avoids any similar insect thereafter. This is no advantage, of course, to the insect that was eaten; the advantage is to the population. Clearly this sort of protection will be more effective if the predator can easily learn which insects to avoid. It is common, therefore, for insects relying on distastefulness to be very brightly coloured and conspicuously marked. This warning colouration of distasteful or poisonous insects often consists of contrasting black and yellow or orange stripes or spots.

Three unrelated and harmless insects which gain protection by virtue of their resemblance to wasps. The three mimics are (top to bottom) a Giant hoverfly (Diptera) a wasp beetle (Coleoptera) and a Hornet clear-wing moth (Lepidoptera).

Mimicry. The term mimicry is commonly applied to the resemblance of one animal (the mimic) to another (the model) such that a third animal is deceived into confusing the two. It was noticed in 1862 by H. W. Bates in the Amazon that many palatable species of insects derived protection by virtue of their similarity to unpalatable species. This type of mimicry, often called Batesian mimicry, can be quite complex and has been much studied. The

143

Left: Caterpillars of the Cinnabar moth on their food plant. These insects are distasteful to would-be predators and the effectiveness of this defence is enhanced by the fact that, due to extremely conspicuous colouration of the insect, the predator easily learns to avoid them. This sort of 'warning colouration' commonly consists of contrasting black and yellow markings.

African swallowtail butterfly *Papilio dardanus* has about six different forms of the female which all mimic different distasteful species of butterflies in different parts of Africa. The situation is further complicated by the presence of other species also mimicking the same models. This sort of system can work only if the distasteful models are more numerous than the mimics, otherwise the predators do not learn to associate distastefulness with that particular appearance.

Yet another type of mimicry was noted by Müller in Brazil. In this case a group of often unrelated species, all of which are distasteful, have come to resemble each other. The advantage of this Müllerian mimicry is that whilst every predator may kill several insects before learning that a particular

colour pattern should be avoided, if several species virtually look alike this limits the number of patterns the predators have to learn, and the learning attacks are shared between species.

The mimicry of inedible objects, described earlier in the chapter, is sometimes regarded as Batesian mimicry. It is sometimes suggested that Müllerian mimicry is not mimicry at all since no deception is involved, as all the species are in fact distasteful. However, the margins between the different types of mimicry are blurred because degrees of palatability or distastefulness may vary for different predators,

A caterpillar of the American moth *Antomeris* which bears bunches of stinging spines that burn and irritate the skin of anyone handling them. This insect relies for protection on being unpleasant, and showing it.

144

and it is not always profitable to attempt to put them into categories.

Insect colour. It will be evident that a very important factor in the defence of insects is their use of colour. This is also true of other aspects of the life of insects and contributes in no small measure to the pleasure we derive from them.

The colours we see in insects are usually associated with the outer covering or cuticle and are derived from either or both of two sources. Various pigments may be present in, or just beneath, the cuticle: alternatively the cuticle may be structured in such a way as to produce colour.

The pigments, which are often by-products of metabolism, produce their colours by differentially absorbing light. The brown or black colour of much insect cuticle is due in part to the tanning process but also to the pigment melanin. The bright yellow of the desert locust *Schistocerca* is produced by a substance called β-carotene which also occurs in the silk of the silkmoth and in beeswax. This pigment also contributes to the red colour of ladybirds (Coleoptera). Some pigments are absorbed from plants; the white colour of the marbled white butterfly *Melanargia* is produced by a flavone taken in by the caterpillar from the grass on which it feeds. Pterines and ommochromes are the most widespread insect pigments and are made by the insects themselves. The colours produced by pterines range from the white of the Cabbage white butterfly, to the yellows of the Hymenoptera and the reds of many insect eyes. Ommochromes are yellow, red or brown and also occur in insect eyes.

The effects of surface structures on light can produce whites, blues and irridescent colours. If light is reflected in all directions by fine granules on or just beneath the surface, the appearance of white is given. This occurs on the surface of the wing scales of some butterflies. If the granules are very small and

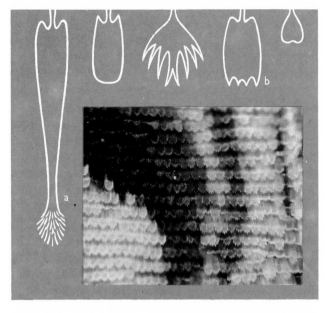

Portion of a butterfly's wing showing scales, overlapping like tiles on a roof, and five variations, shown in outline, in the many shapes scales can assume, according to species.

regularly spaced, with dimensions similar to the wavelength of blue light, the surface appears blue. This so-called Tyndall blue is rare in insects but the blue of dragonflies is produced in this way.

Quite often the scales of butterflies, the elytra of beetles, or the membranous wings of other insects are composed of layers of transparent cuticle with very small spaces between them. The spaces between these reflecting layers are similar in dimension to the wavelength of particular colours. These colours are reflected, whilst others in the impinging light are extinguished by a process called interference. As you look at the insect from different angles you alter the effective distance between the reflecting layers and so the colour changes. This phenomenon is known as irridescence and accounts for some of the most beautiful colourings in insects.

The occasions when the life of insects and the life of man impinge on each other are numerous. Insects are often admired or cursed but seldom ignored. So it is that on the basis of their relation to man, insects can be regarded as beneficial or harmful. Just as it is part of human nature to take for granted the advantageous and complain about the inconvenient, so most of us, even the entomologists, are much more aware of and preoccupied with the injurious insects and their effects than with the beneficial ones. Nevertheless, without insects our lives would be radically altered to our advantage as well as to our disadvantage. Let us finally take a brief look at some of the ways in which we would be affected.

Pollination. Many present day plants such as grasses, cereals and most trees are wind pollinated. On the other hand, most orchard fruits, many market vegetables, field crops like clover, cotton and tobacco, and most flowers depend entirely on insects for their pollination and continued existence. Insects, particularly bees, collect pollen for food but in doing so transfer appreciable quantities from one flower to another where some of it reaches the female structures and effects fertilization. Many flowers have peculiar features of structure that help to ensure pollination and frequently nectar is pro-

duced as an added attractant; the conspicuous colours and patterns of flowers which so delight our eyes have evolved really for the eye of the insect. Plants such as honeysuckle and tobacco, having strongly scented nocturnal flowers, are pollinated not only by bees but by certain moths as well.

The role of honey-bees in fruit orchards is now widely recognized and most growers obtain substantially increased yields of fruit by keeping hives of bees in their orchards while the trees are in bloom. Experiments involving cages over orchard trees have shown that if bees are excluded, the set of fruit is less than 1 % of the blooms, while with bees present it is up to 44 %. Some years ago sheep farmers in New Zealand imported red clover seed to improve their pastures. The clover grew but it set no seed until bumble bees had been introduced and established.

Commercial Products. Bees have been husbanded ever since the time of the Pharaohs and honey is used extensively today as a food and in the manufacture of many other products. Beeswax is also widely used in industry, in the manufacture of candles, sealing wax, polishes and some kinds of ink. In the United States there are estimated to be about 6 million colonies of honey-bees producing 240 million lb (100 million kg) of honey and 4·5 million lb (2 mil-

A bumblebee on clover with its pollen baskets (the yellow protuberance on each hindleg) filled. Bumblebees are particularly valuable as pollinators of clover and other flowers.

side.

lion kg) of wax annually – a multimillion-dollar industry.

The principally oriental industry of silk production is similarly ancient, extending back to 2500 BC. The silk is obtained from the cocoon of a silk moth, now chiefly *Bombyx mori*, a domesticated species. Despite the introduction of various synthetic fibres, the silk industry is still a flourishing one.

Another commercial product of importance is shellac, obtained from the secretions of the Lac insect *Laccifer lacca* which is a scale insect occurring on fig, banyan and other plants in South East Asia. Another scale insect which lives on prickly pear gives us the red dye cochineal. It takes 70,000 insects to make 1 lb (0·45 kg) of dye.

Various Beneficial Activities. We have seen that insects have a tremendous reproductive capacity and they can very easily achieve pest status if environmental factors suddenly favour them. A major check on such insects is exerted by other predatory and parasitic insects; probably nothing that man can do in controlling insects by other methods can compare with the control exerted by insects themselves. This has been exploited by man in a number of cases, a notable example being the control of the scale insect *Icerya purchasi*, which was threatening the survival of the citrus industry in California, by the introduction of ladybird beetles to eat them.

Insects can also be of great value in destroying undesirable plants. The prickly pear cactus was introduced into Australia and spread rapidly to form a dense impenetrable cover. But in 1925 a moth, *Cactoblastis cactorum*, the larvae of which burrow in the cactus, was introduced from Argentina. Almost unbelievably the caterpillars cleared about 25 million acres (100,000 sq km) in only two years and have kept the cactus confined ever since to an area about 1% of that which it occupied in 1925.

The balance of pest and predator, leaving neither utterly defeated, is vitally important in control. It is virtually impossible to eradicate a pest completely; this is partly because when its numbers decrease to a level at which it is no longer economically important it attracts less attention. It is arguably best to leave a fair population of a potential pest so that there will always be reserves of its predators and parasites available against the possibility of a sudden increase in pest numbers. The application of insecticides sometimes does more harm to the predators than the pest. This is not to suggest that insecticides should not be used; indeed at the present time there is no substitute for the use of insecticides. One merely hopes that they are used with care and real effort to monitor their effects on the prey/predator/parasite interactions which are so complex that they are seldom completely understood.

A silk moth cocoon cut open to show the pupa inside.

The Burying beetle *Necrophorus humator* on the carcass of a Pigmy shrew. These beetles bury the corpses of small mammals and birds on which they lay their eggs. The larvae from these feed on the decaying flesh.

148

A selection of the many forms of invertebrates, most of them microscopic or near-microscopic, making up the soil fauna: (1) spring-tail *Tomoceros longicornis*; (2) proturan *Protentomon thienmanni*; (3) earthworm; (4) centipede *Necrophloeophagus longicornis*; (5) bristle-tail *Campodea staphylinos*; (6) springtail *Folsomia quadricolata*; (7) mite *Oppia quadricarinata*; (8) pauropod *Pauropus huxleyi*; (9) tardigrade *Echiniscus quadrispinosus*; (10) beetle larva *Agriotes obscurus*; (11) springtail *Onychiurusdebilis* and (12) mite *Oribotritia loricata*.

Another vitally important but little understood group are the soil insects and scavengers, hastening the breakdown of dead organic material and so speeding the return of nutrients to the soil. As well as adding to its organic content, soil animals improve the physical properties of the soil, especially by tunnelling in it in such a way that it is well aerated. The tunnels of wood-boring insects serve as avenues of entrance for fungi and bacteria which hasten the conversion of fallen trees to humus. Carrion-eating insects such as blowflies, carrion beetles and skin beetles, remove carrion from the landscape while dung beetles and dung flies do the same with dung. When cattle were introduced into Australia, there were no dung beetles so the dung dried and persisted for years, making large areas of pasture useless. The balance of nature was restored only when dung beetles were introduced from other parts of the world.

Insects form an important source of food for a great number of animals. These include many fish, game birds and mammals which are themselves important sources of food for man. In many parts of the world insects are used directly as food for man. In Africa, ants, termites, beetle larvae, caterpillars and grasshoppers are eaten; in Arabian countries locusts are eaten, and grasshoppers are a common food in parts of the Orient. In Mexico, the large caterpillars of one of the giant skipper butterflies are considered a delicacy. They are sold in markets and fried before eating, or they can be bought in cans, already fried and ready to serve. Cans of these and other edible insects are available in many Western countries.

Insects have been used for centuries in medicine and surgery. Some urinogenital diseases have been treated with cantharidin, an extract from blister beetles; bee venom has been used in the treatment of arthritis. It was noted in the sixteenth century, and more fully exploited during World War I, that wounds healed more effectively after they had been invaded by blowfly larvae. Maggots were used in the treatment of stubborn ulcers and of osteomyelitis. The curative value of living maggots was subsequently traced to one of their excretory products, allantoin and this was used until ousted by modern antibiotics.

The beauty of insects has inspired artists, jewellers and designers for millennia. The wing cases of beetles were used in the ornamentation of Oriental temples in ancient times; the black, white and red pattern of the leafhopper *Cardioscarta* is a recurring motif in the art of Mexico and Central America; the brilliant iridescent blue wings of *Morpho* butterflies

Juniper 'big bud' gall opened to show the midge larva inside. It is not until the larva hatches out from the egg that damage to the bud occurs.

Top left: Bean gall on willow caused by the sawfly *Pontania proxima*. Top right: Rose bedeguar or Robin's pincushion is common on wild roses in Europe. Bottom left: Galls on roots of oak caused by larvae of unisexual generation of Gall wasp *Biorhiza pallida*. Bottom right: Oak apple gall caused by larvae of the bisexual generation of the Gall wasp *Biorhiza pallida*.

Female Gall midge *Schmidtiella gemmarum* the cause of 'big bud' on juniper shrubs, by laying her eggs, three of which are shown here beside her, in the buds.

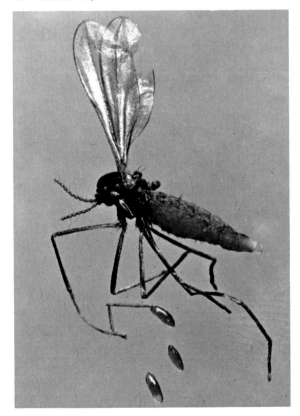

of South America have a recurring fascination for the designers of jewelry, trays and pictures.

Insects as Crop Pests. Virtually all man's crop plants are susceptible to injury caused by insects feeding or ovipositing on the plants or acting as vectors in the transmission of plant diseases. The economic losses may be enormous; in the United States alone over 125 species of insects attack cotton, causing an annual loss estimated in 1970 at over 200 million dollars.

Leaf eaters can at worst defoliate a plant and kill it, at best they reduce its photosynthetic tissue and diminish its productivity. Similar effects are produced by insects sucking the sap and producing wilting, or feeding in tunnels which may be bored in virtually any part of the plant. Woolly aphids and the soil-dwelling larvae of various beetles and flies feed on roots, damaging such crops as cabbage, corn and grasses.

Many plant-feeding insects inject a chemical into the plant which causes it to grow abnormally and produce a gall which protects the feeding insect inside it. The chemical is usually produced by the insect in the gall but sometimes it is injected by the

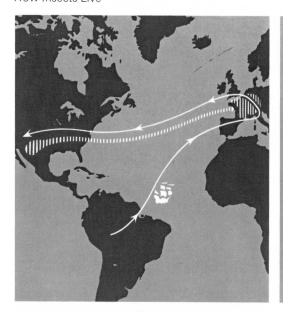

Left: Map showing how the potato was taken from South America to Europe and thence to North America. The Colorado beetle was introduced to Europe from the United States in the 1920's. Centre: The life history of the beetle, showing the larva and pupa. Right: The adult with its characteristic stripes.

adult female as she lays her eggs in the plant. Apart from this, insects such as the periodical cicada may cause considerable physical damage during oviposition, even causing the twig concerned to die and drop off.

About 200 plant diseases have been shown to be transmitted by insects and three-quarters of them are caused by viruses carried mainly by Homoptera. The disease-causing organism or pathogen may enter the plant accidentally through wounds made by insects. Alternatively it may be carried on or in the body of the insect from one plant to another. The fungus causing Dutch elm disease is transmitted in this way by the Elm bark beetle. Sometimes, as with a wilt disease of cucumbers, the pathogen spends part of its life cycle in the body of the insect and may reproduce there. Occasionally the pathogen passes from the insect to its offspring through the eggs.

Stored Product Pests. Even when a crop has been harvested it is not free from attack. Plant and animal products stored for use as food or converted into fabrics or buildings may be damaged by insects feeding or tunnelling in them, often contaminating them in the process. The worst offenders are various beetles and moths which attack grains, pulses and flour, termites and wood-boring beetles, clothes moths, skin beetles and the larvae of various flies. Grain is particularly susceptible to attack; it is estimated that 5–10% of the world's grain production is damaged by insects during storage and this may rise to 50% in the tropics.

Cottonstainers, which are long legged bugs, are notorious pests of cotton. Top: First instar larvae a few hours old with some eggs. Centre: Fourth instar larvae. Bottom: Two adults in final mating posture.

152

A plant stem containing eggs of the Green bush-cricket *Conocephalus discolor*. The eggs of bush-crickets are sometimes laid in the soil but more often in or on the stems or leaves of plants.

One of the insect scourges, in Britain at least, is the Death-watch beetle *Xestobium rufovillosum*, which has eaten into the timbers of ancient buildings such as cathedrals, causing extensive damage.

153

A Timber beetle, or Longhorn beetle *Acanthophorus maculatus* of Nigeria. The Longhorn beetles are so called because of their long antennae. They are found throughout the world where trees or bushes grow or wherever timber is transported or used.

Insects Attacking Man and His Animals. In some localities we experience much annoyance from the attentions of midges, mosquitoes and other biting or stinging insects whose venoms may cause irritation, swelling, pain or even death to people who have become sensitized. Domestic animals are similarly affected and these insects, and others like face flies and bot flies which neither bite nor sting but greatly annoy cattle, may be the direct cause of reduced yield of meat or milk.

Similar effects are produced by a wide range of parasitic insects which live in or on the bodies of man and his animals. Fleas, lice and various blood-sucking bugs cause irritation, and a general run-down condition; sometimes bad sores result from scratching brought on by their bites. The larvae of many flies live as internal parasites, infesting and destroying tissues and causing a condition known as myiasis, which is extremely debilitating and sometimes deadly.

The most serious effect of insect attack on man and animals is caused by those insects which act as vectors for diseases. As with plant diseases, the pathogens may be transmitted 'accidentally' by the insects, or alternatively, the insect may act as a host in the life cycle of the pathogen. Houseflies and

154

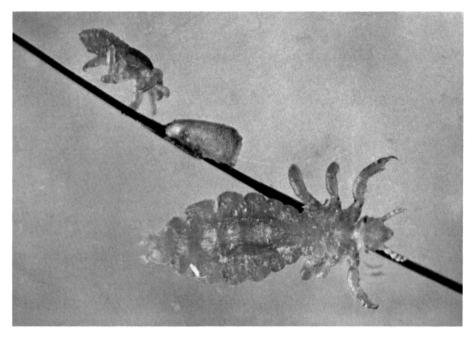

A human head louse with an immature individual and an egg attached to a hair. Human lice can thrive in unclean conditions where there is lack of personal hygiene and can transmit the diseases known as typhus and relapsing fever.

blowflies, which frequent carrion, excrement and filth of all sorts, are notorious for contaminating man's food with germs. Not only do they spread germs as they walk on our food but, in the process of feeding on it, they regurgitate onto it materials that were previously eaten by them. Dysentery, cholera and typhoid fever may be transmitted in this way.

Those insects which serve as hosts as well as

A Tse-tse fly cleaning its proboscis after feeding on the photographer.

155

A sheep ked, an insect with degenerate wings, which lives in the fleece and sucks the sheep's blood.

vectors for the pathogen are usually blood-suckers. The pathogen, a virus, bacterium, protozoon or parasitic worm, is carried by the insect and injected into the man or animal, usually during feeding. In this way malaria, elephantiasis, yellow fever and dengue are spread by mosquitoes; sleeping sickness and nagana by tsetse flies; various forms of typhus and relapsing fever by lice; bubonic plague by fleas; kala-azar, Oriental sore and various fevers by sandflies; Chagas' disease by assassin bugs; anthrax by horseflies. Malaria, perhaps the most important of all human diseases and caused by the protozoon parasite *Plasmodium*, is transmitted by mosquitoes of the genus *Anopheles*. It is estimated that there are about 250 million cases of malaria in the world every year and about 3 million of these are fatal.

It seems a pity to end on a note of conflict between ourselves and the insects. But we should remember as we attempt to master this planet and adapt its resources to our own ends, that the unreasoning force of evolution is driving the insects to do the same in different ways, so that conflict is inevitable. Nor should we forget that evolution had been moulding the lives of insects before we arrived on this planet, for a time-span longer than we can properly imagine. I fancy that the insects will still be here when the artifacts of man are mouldering in obscurity.

Mosquitoes and disease. (1) the Common mosquito *Culex pipiens*, (2) the Malarial mosquito *Anopheles maculpennis* and (3) the same seen in side view to show how its abdomen is tilted upwards when the insect is at rest. (4) The Yellow fever mosquito *Aedes aegypti*. (5) human blood corpuscles infected with the Malarial parasite *Plasmodium vivax*. First a cell containing a trophozoite breaks up into merozoites that are liberated into the blood. It is at this stage that antidotes to malaria can be effective, before the merozoites re-enter other corpuscles to assume the sickle-shape and start the cycle all over again. (6) Common mosquito at rest, with body horizontal. (7) A larva and (8) a pupa of this mosquito, both aquatic, breathing, suspended from the surface film. Two Common mosquitoes, one (9) feeding and one (10) gorged with blood. (11) The Yellow fever mosquito, resting, seen in side view, with the body horizontal. (12) The large but harmless Crane fly *Tipula gigantea*. (13) The small blackfly *Melusina maculata* and (14) the midge *Clytocerus ocellaris*, relatives of the mosquitoes.

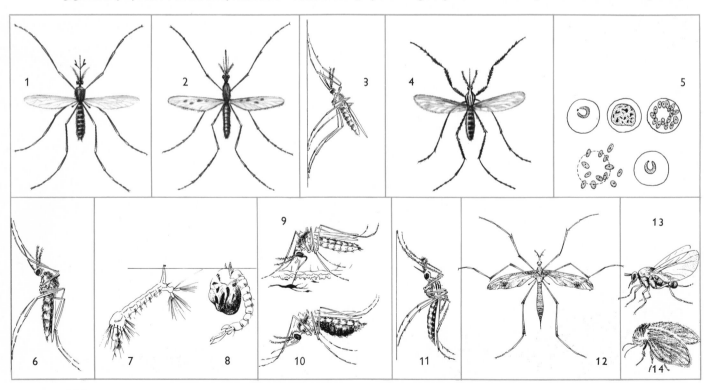

Index

Italics are used for generic and specific names and also to indicate pages on which illustrations appear.

159

Index